20th-CENTURY REMINISCENCE SERIES

When Elvis Presley entered Baptist Memorial Hospital in January of 1975, Marian Cocke, a Unit Supervisor placed in charge of his nursing program, little realized how her life would change. Soon she was serving on a voluntary basis at Graceland, not only administering his prescription medication program, but also serving as a friend and confidante.

Many times they talked all night, and Elvis never left Graceland without stopping by to tell her good-bye. With him she shared exciting trips; from him she received fabulous gifts. Together they laughed and cried both at his difficulties and good fortune and at her own.

In this candid and warm reminiscence, published with the encouragement of Vernon Presley, Marian Cocke tells of the man she called "Babe": she describes his medications, tells of his diet, discusses his deeply religious nature and shows his love of his family, his sense of humor, and his lonliness. This is a loving and tender book that shows the Elvis Presley too few people were able to know and will be cherished by those who loved the man who said only Christ should be called "The King".

ABOUT THE AUTHOR

Marian Elizabeth Justice Cocke was born on July 28, 1926, at Fort Benning, Georgia, to Howard and Nocal Justice, and was one of five children. Born and raised an "Army Brat," she was not accustomed to civilian life until she began attending Whitehave High School in Memphis in 1942, graduating from itin 1943. In 1946 she entered The Holy Name of Jesus Hospital Training School for nurses in Gadsden, Alabama and graduated in 1949.

Three years later, on September 13, 1952, she married Robert Andrew Cocke of Clarksdale, Mississippi, and on October 12, 1953, their only child, Catherine Elizabeth (Katey), was born. Mrs. Cocke began work at Baptist Memorial Hospital in Memphis on May 9, 1969, as an Infusion Nurse and later became unit supervisor. She still is an employee of that institution in her present capacity as Administrative Supervisor in Nursing Services.

Because of her strong feelings against makin money from her friendship with one she loved, she hesitated about having her memoirs become public knowledge. However, after talking with Vernon Presley, Elvis' father, she was persuaded to allow her manuscript to be published, for it would be of interest to Elvis' fans and would give insights into the sort of man Elvis really was.

Mrs. Cocke has already decided where she will donate her royalties from this book: the suite which he last occupied in the hospital will be memorialized in his name, some will be given to the cancer research program at Baptist Memorial Hospital in Memphis, some to her church, some to Forget-Me-Not, Incorporated and to others.

I CALLED
HIM BABE:
ELVIS PRESLEY'S NURSE REMEMBERS

By

Marian J. Cocke

For ELVIS AARON PRESLEY,
a gentleman and a gentle man;

And for my mother, NOCAL ELIZABETH JUSTICE,
a queen in the eyes of her family;

And in appreciation of BOB and KATEY,
*who, by their unselfish and understanding
nature, made it possible for me to know
and love the boy I called Babe.*

CONTENTS

1.   I Meet Elvis

*I*n January of 1975 I was the unit supervisor on 18 Madison East at the Baptist Memorial Hospital in Memphis, Tennessee. The first of January I guess was like all other Januarys I have seen come and go. Christmas was several days gone, Dick and his family had gone back to Mississippi, Catherine and her clan had gone back to Texas, Joe to Virginia and the rest of us—Mother, Daddy and Patty, and me, and my family—had settled down into the routine of everyday living.

Sometime during the second week of January, a good friend, Dr. George Nichopolus, dropped by the nursing station and asked to speak to me for a few minutes. Dr. Nick, as we called him, was the personal physician of Elvis Presley. He told me that Elvis had been sick for several days, and he wanted to bring him into the hospital if he could talk him into coming; he said that Elvis really didn't want to come, so Dr. Nick was having a little difficulty convincing him that he should. We had a suite available on my unit which Dr. Nick asked if I could hold at least for a few days. I called my good friend, Sara Edwards. She was in charge of "bed central," and I knew I could keep her confidence so I explained why I wanted the suite "tied up" so no one else would get it.

Only a day or two had gone by when Dr. Nick came back and said that Elvis would be coming in sometime that night or early the next morning. I asked if there was anything special that I should do, and I was asked to cover the windows with foil to keep out the daylight and to move another bed into the suite. I did what was asked of me. Dr. Nick then asked me if I would be there the next day; when I told him that I was off that day, he asked if I would come in and stay with Elvis, saying he would call me when they left Graceland so I could meet them at the hospital. I agreed to do this.

When I came home from the hospital and told Bob, my husband, and Katey, my daughter, that I was going in during the night or early morning to stay with Elvis, they were both pleased, and Katey, understandably, was really excited! I called Mother, Daddy, and Patty, and they too were pleased that I had been asked to go in.

That night when I went to bed, I was so excited I couldn't sleep. I think I stayed awake all night, watching the clock and waiting for the phone to ring. Around 5 a.m. the expected call came. Dr. Nick was saying that they would be leaving from Graceland in the next few minutes. I jumped up and dressed and took off from home in a hurry — I was so excited!

When I arrived at the hospital, from the time I walked in the door, everything seemed different. There were few people about at that time of the morning, and yet there was an aura of excitement in the air. Maybe it was just me, but everything felt different.

I got up on 18 Madison East, and the night duty nurses were buzzing about with excitement. There was a hospital security guard standing in front of the nurses' station, and when I looked down the hall toward the suite, there were two guards at the door and several others were milling about. I took my coat to my office and then headed toward the suite. As I write this, I can still feel the anticipation as I literally danced down that hall.

I need to pause here and say that I had never really been an Elvis fan; I had seen him on a previous admission many years ago, and had even walked down the hall with him, talking as we walked and without the fanfare of any bodyguards. It is very difficult for me to get excited about someone I do not know, and yet, this particular day and time, I really felt "different." Perhaps it was because I had been asked personally to come and stay with him that day. I really can't say what it was. Maybe magic.

I walked into the room, which was very dimly lit; I soon learned that Elvis did not like a lot of lights on. The room was full of men: Vernon Presley, Joe Esposito, Al Strada, Dr. Nick, and others; Linda Thompson also was there. Dr. Nick introduced me to each person, saving the best for last; there, sitting on the bed in a pair of navy blue nylon pajamas, sporting a beard and with a shock of black hair falling over his left eye, sat a boy who walked right into my heart. He smiled and said, "Hello." Dr. Nick asked me laughingly if I knew who he was, and I said, "I know who this is." A few pleasantries were exchanged, after which all of the fellows, along with Vernon, said it was time for them to go. Joe Esposito suggested private duty nurses, which Elvis promptly vetoed (he had always had them in the past when he was hospitalized), so everyone left except Linda and Al Strada. I asked if anyone was hungry, but they had all eaten before coming to the hospital. Al was sleepy and so was Linda.

I excused myself from the room and went out to the dietary unit to get water (lots of ice water!) and orange juice and to check on what medications had been ordered from the pharmacy. When I got back to the suite with my armload of necessary items, Elvis was sitting up in the middle of his bed, and Linda had just finished shaving him. He grinned at me once again and asked me to sit down.

We spent the next hour getting acquainted — what any two people would do after just meeting. Linda had left, and Elvis and I sat and swapped family stories. I was really afraid that he might feel that I expected to be entertained, so I suggested that he might like to go to sleep. I said I would go across the hall to the sitting room and be within earshot if he should need me. He said, "Oh, Mrs. Cocke, please just sit here and talk to me; it's very seldom that I can ever sit and talk to just plain real people, and I'd like to just visit if it's okay with you." Well, of course, nothing could have pleased me more, and we sat for eight hours and talked; we spoke of nothing in particular other than our families, but we pretty much touched on a lot in general.

From the start Elvis called me "Miss" Cocke, although hereafter I will write it "Mrs." Most Southerners pronounce the word "Miss," and he always called me "Miss" Cocke.

He really did not want to talk show business, and only touched on it briefly to speak of his tremendous respect for John Wayne and Mary Tyler Moore. The visit was interrupted from time to time long enough for me to go out for frequent pitchers of ice water and glasses of orange juice. Each time I went out to the nursing station for these things, I was always hit with many questions — "What does he look like?" "Is he as handsome as his pictures?" "Is he nice?" "Is he asleep?" and mainly, "Would you like for me to stay with him so you can go to lunch?" I had more offers for relief than Carter had liver pills! Everyone was "considerate" in wanting to give me a "break" from my duty. Other people tried to get by the guard at the door that day, but he kept in close contact with me so that no one got in.

During the course of that day, Elvis asked me, as I was the floor supervisor, how I intended to plan for his care and if I wanted him to have private duty nurses. I asked which he preferred, and he said he would leave that up to me, but that he wanted me to take care of him regardless of who else was involved. Between the two of us, we decided that I would take care of him on the 7-3 shift and that the charge nurses on the shifts from 3-11 and 11-7 would take care of him during their respective shifts. A list of these nurses would be given to the guard each day by 1:00 p.m., and only these nurses would be allowed in the room. No other floor personnel or personnel from other areas would enter the suite unless the guard at the door checked with me.

During the next three weeks there were many, many hospital workers who tried, including some of the house physicians, without success, to invade the compound; there was even a couple of doctors that Dr. Nick mentioned to me that he was sending by that the guard refused to let in unless I gave the okay, so we really had a tight security system established.

The 3-11 p.m. nurse in charge, except on her days off, was a fairly new graduate from the University of Arkansas, and she was as cute as a button. The 11-7 (night) nurse was a graduate of Memphis State University. The 3-11 nurse was vivacious, while the other nurse was shy and only spoke when spoken to. This nursing arrangement worked out well as far as the 7-3 and 3-11 shifts were concerned, but because of her extreme shyness, Elvis felt uncomfortable with the night nurse and asked if there perhaps was another nurse who could be assigned to him from 11-7. There was an LPN (licensed practical nurse) who worked at the unit during these hours; she was a very outgoing person. Elvis was pleased that he now had his twenty-four hour "talking service" established. This arrangement lasted for the remainder of the three weeks that he was hospitalized. He and I continued to spend as much time as possible just chatting, but I had responsibilities to the other fifty patients on the floor and to the institution, and I felt very strongly about my obligations. This Elvis respected. He was never, in any way, demanding of my time, but actually appeared grateful for any time I could spend with him.

As I have previously stated, many people wanted to get in to see the "King of Rock and Roll," including my twenty-one-year-old daughter, Katey. She had an appointment with her doctor one day, and she came by the floor to see me. She was sitting in my office talking to Dr. Bob Tate, a favorite young medical resident, and I went in and told her not to leave the floor until I checked with her. Actually I had told Elvis that I needed to see Katey before she left the floor, and he asked me to bring her in to see him before she left. I told him that this really would not be fair to the personnel because they also wanted to see him, and he said, "Yes, but I want her to come in." When Katey and Bob Tate finished their conversation, she came out to the nurses' station to ask why I wanted her, and I led her down the hall toward Elvis' room and told her that he wanted to meet her. Was she ever excited! Mercy, you've never seen a happier girl!

When we went into the foyer of the suite, I had Katey wait while I called Elvis from the sitting room. He had gone in to sit with Al, David Leech, and David Stanley. As he came into the foyer, Katey just stood there in awe and with tears in her eyes. Elvis took one of her hands, kissed her on the cheek, and said, "Hello, honey, how are you?"

Katey replied, "Fine, thank you, sir. How are you?"

We went into the suite's bedroom and sat for probably ten or fifteen minutes. I am sure those ten or fifteen minutes were the shortest minutes in her young life. I reminded her that she had to go see Dr. Simmons, so as we got up to leave, Elvis got up, put his arm around her shoulders, and once again kissed her on the cheek. Katey didn't walk out of that room — she floated. It was such a big day for her, and what a happy surprise.

Various tests and X-rays took place in the days that followed after Elvis had had several good days of rest. He was an excellent patient and was most cooperative in all the procedures. One day during one of our many visits, Elvis told me that he would like to give each of us (the three nurses taking care of him) a present before he went home, and did I think a pin or a necklace or a ring would be okay? I told him that it had been so much fun taking care of him, which had been my pleasure, that it would be spoiled if he turned around and did something for me, at least as far as I was concerned, so please not to give me anything. I remember thinking he would be on the "receiving end" this once rather than on the giving. Little did I know!

One morning at seven a.m., when I went on duty, the night nurse in giving the morning report, said that a liver biopsy had been ordered for that a.m. and was to be done early by Dr. Lawrence Wruble. She told me that everything was in the room, so, after I went through my morning routine, I went to the suite to check on supplies for the biopsy. Elvis was awake, and I explained the procedure which was to follow. Dr. Wruble came in within the next few minutes, and the liver biopsy was performed. I had the ice cap ready for the injection site and had Elvis turn to his right side. Dr. Wruble left the room and Elvis asked me to go in the sitting room and get Al. I got Al, then began removing the equipment from the room; Elvis asked Al to come over to the bedside table and get something out of the drawer for him. I started to leave, but Elvis asked me to wait, so I stepped to the back of the room.

I could only see Al's back, but I knew that he said to Elvis, "Just any one?" Elvis replied, "No, just open them until I see it. I know which one I want." Al opened two boxes before Elvis said, "That's it." Then Al stepped back, and Elvis asked me to come over to the bed. He was holding a small black satin box which, as he opened it, he said, "Mrs. Cocke, I have a little gift for you."

When I saw what my "little gift" was, my knees turned to water. There, in the box, was the most beautiful gold filigreed cross I had ever seen. It had thirteen diamonds in it, and certainly it was more elegant than anything I had ever seen or expected to own. It had tiny flecks of black onyx surrounding the diamonds. It is truly a magnificent piece of jewelry. Naturally, I cried, and, as I thanked him, he said, "You're very welcome," and kissed me on the cheek. He asked if I preferred a chain so I could wear it as a necklace; I preferred the chain and was presented with one which actually looks like tiny gold chains braided together. It is very beautiful.

After he gave me my necklace, he told me that he knew that he was going home, probably the next day, and that he wanted to give me something before he left. He said he had given the 3-11 nurse a ring the night before, and he also had a gift for the 11-7 nurse, but as she was off duty, he would give her hers that night when she came to work. The day he gave me my gift was Valentine's Day, 1975. My personnel on the floor had given me a white carnation corsage with small red hearts on it, and they said that his gift made theirs look sick. I told them that theirs was given with love and was as precious a gift as the cross was.

The next stop I made was to show my beautiful gift to Janet Stroud, my then immediate boss, Miss Farnell, director of nursing service, Diana Baker, associate director of nursing service, and all of the other ladies in the nursing office. Everyone was pleased for me.

As Elvis was about ready for discharge, it was decided to have a surgeon come in and check out his colon so Dr. John Nash was asked to come by. I had known this young man since he was an intern and resident, and had a particular fondness for him, I guess because I felt like I helped "raise him." You develop a fondness for these fellows who come in as "boys" and you watch them mature and become "men." Dr. Nash did examine him, and any type of possible colon surgery was ruled out. He then stopped by the nurses' station and wanted to see my gift. His reaction was, "Gosh, I've never seen anything so fabulous."

When I got home that night and showed my gift to Bob and Katey, they also were pleased. Katey cried because Elvis had given me such a lovely gift. She had bought him a gift of very expensive after shaving lotion, and she asked me if I would take it to him. I asked why she had gotten him a gift, and she said, "Because he was so nice to see me." I took her gift to work with me the next day and put it in my desk drawer. I knew that he would go home that night, and I was going to wait until I went off duty to give it to him. The 11-7 nurse came bounding into my office to show me her gift, which was a small, delicate cross studded with tiny diamonds on a delicate gold chain; she was so excited she could hardly contain herself. She asked if she could see my gift, which I had on beneath my uniform. I drew the chain from around my neck to show her. She gasped and said she had never seen anything so lovely. She left to go home, and another day started.

During the morning, around 10:00, Elvis called and asked if I would come down to his room so that he could talk to me. When I went down, he presented me with a gold and diamond cross for Katey and asked if I would take it to her. I told him that she had sent him a gift which I had planned to give him that day when I left at the end of my shift, so I went out and got it for him. She had written him a note thanking him for seeing her, wishing him well, and telling him how she appreciated his kindness to her and to her mother. Elvis appeared quite touched.

Around 2:30 that afternoon, the 3-11 nurse came on duty and had a big smile on her face and a gorgeous ring on her finger. I said how beautiful her ring was, and she asked what he had given me. Once again I tugged at the gold chain around my neck, and when she saw the cross, she reacted as Linda had done that morning. The thing most touching to me was that each of us thought our gift was the loveliest.

All of the jewelry came from Harry Levitch's jewelry store. Elvis was very fond of the Levitches and held them in high regard. He told me that most of the jewelry he bought came from these people.

That night, after the hospital was quiet and the visitors had left the building, Elvis went home—and the magic was gone! The coach turned back into a pumpkin, the white horses became mice, and the fairy princess once again became plain old "Mrs. Cocke." I realized this the next morning when I got to work and looked down the hall to see the door to the suite standing open. The young man who had spent three weeks in that room had touched my life in a way that I had not realized until he left.

Later, after Elvis had left the hospital, I was visiting with a friend one day. We were talking about my famous patient. She asked me how I had gotten along with him, was he easy to take care of, what he called me, etc. Before I left her that day, she asked if he had given me a gift, and I told her that he had given me a diamond cross necklace, and I showed it to her as I was wearing it under my clothing. She agreed that it was truly beautiful, but then she added, "You know, they say that he gives a car to the people he really cares about."

I was flabbergasted, but I came back with, "Oh, you're wrong. A car will wear out, but he was so fond of me that he gave me something that will last forever!"

Many months later, long after he had given me a car, I told Elvis about that comment. He remarked, "You're exactly right, I give away lot of cars, but when I give someone a cross, they are very special to me."

I don't think most people realize how religious Elvis was. He was very close to God. He knew that his talent was given to him by God, and he wanted to return to God what was rightfully His. I think that one way he did this was by the many benefits he did and the many people he helped on an individual basis.

2. Elvis And His Thoughtfulness

The day before Elvis left the hospital, just after the 3-11 nurse and I had admired each other's gift, she asked if she could speak to me in private. We went into my office where she told me that Elvis had asked her to work for him, go on tour with him, and leave her job at the hospital. She was extremely excited about the opportunity and said that she wanted to give me her letter of resignation. I told her that I could certainly see and understand her excitement, but cautioned her to give a lot of thought and prayer to her decision. She had been dating Al Strada since she had first met him, and I reminded her that she would be in a completely different life style, that she was young and impressionable, and that I thought she should certainly give a lot of thought to her decision, talk to her parents about it, and that, whatever she decided, I wished her well. In speaking to her, I asked if I could hold her letter of resignation until she spoke to her parents, and she said, "Well, okay, but my mind is pretty much made up." She, knowing that my Katey was her age, asked how I would feel about my own child taking such a job, and I told her that I would hate to see her make a hasty decision.

The next morning she was still excited. She definitely had decided to make the change and go to work for Elvis, and was busy shopping and tying up loose ends. Elvis had given her a thousand dollars to buy new clothes with, and she was really getting things in order. Dr. Nick came to me and asked if I had any influence over her; I told him that I had talked to her, but that she was determined to leave. She had asked me for a couple of days off so she could go to Arkansas to see her parents; Dr. Nick wanted to call her while she was home to see if he could persuade her to change her mind — to no avail.

Several days later, on a Sunday night, I received a phone call at home from Dr. Nick. He said that Vernon Presley had had a heart attack, and he wanted to put him in the suite on my floor. I called the floor to let the girls know that he would be coming in and to get things ready: a monitor and 02 (oxygen) set up. An hour or so later, Dr. Nick called back to say that Vernon was in the room and comfortable. Dr. Nick was going to have a nurse from his office stay with him that night until 11 p.m., and could I get a nurse to come in at 11:00 to stay with him. I called a nurse who at one time had worked on my unit and who since had gone to work in the ICU (intensive care unit) department. She was an excellent cardiac nurse, and she agreed to stay with Vernon that night when she got off duty at 11 p.m.

The next day when I went to work, I checked on Vernon, and he was doing fine. He was getting nasal 02, and was on the monitor, which indicated that he was stabilized. He also was a good patient and was as undemanding as Elvis had been. And he too was a very pleasant person.

While Vernon was there, my mother was admitted to the hospital for a checkup because of her diverticulitis. My mother's name was Nocal Justice, and she was in the room right next door to the suite. She had been given a series of tests. Little did she know that the last night she was to remain in the hospital would be an exciting time for her, but I'll tell you about that in a few minutes.

That day I had been in a meeting that had lasted nearly three hours. It was the 27th of February; the last day to work was February 28th for the 3-11 nurse who had been offered the job with Elvis. We had planned a cake and a party for her, and I had gone to the gift shop and gotten her a nice gift from the floor; we were going to have the party her last day on the floor. Anyway, on the 27th, when I got back to the floor, I went immediately to Mother's room to see if the reports were in on her tests. As they were not, I decided that I would stay that night until her doctor, Leigh Adkins, a close personal friend, came in to give us her report. I went to the nurses' station and was given a note to call Joe Esposito as soon as possible. I recognized the number as being one of the private lines at Graceland. When my call was put through to Joe, his first question to me was, "Can she stay at the hospital, or is her resignation final?" I asked what was going on, and he said that it had been decided by the California office that it was a mistake to hire a nurse as it might project an image that Elvis was really sick and had to have a nurse with him because of poor health. When I got off the phone, she was standing nearby. Although she looked at me quizzically, she asked me no questions, and I offered no answers to her questioning look.

As my shift on duty had ended, I locked up my office and went down the hall to Mother's room and confided to her the phone call I had just received from Joe. She asked me how I felt about the decision, and I told her that I knew that she would be hurt and terribly disappointed, but hopefully she would realize that this was actually the best thing that could happen to her. I remained in Mother's room until her supper tray was sent in, and while she ate I went downstairs to the drug store for some necessary items and then on to the cafeteria.

When I returned to the floor, she was at the desk and the moment I looked at her face I knew that she had been told. Her face was tear-stained, her eyes were swollen, and she was furious. She glared at me as I went down the hall to deposit my purchases in Mother's room, and I got the keys to my office and said I would be back shortly. When I got to the nurses' station, I told her that I wanted to see her in my office. She was so angry that I knew she didn't want to come, but she did without question. She was so miserable! I asked her to have a seat, and the first thing I said to her then was, "Now cry real good and get it all out of your system." With this, she dissolved in tears, and I felt so sorry for her that I cried with her.

When she finally composed herself, she looked at me and said, "You knew all along, didn't you?"

I told her of the phone call I had received from Joe that afternoon and that he asked me if she could keep her job. I told her what he had said, and that I did not tell her about the conversation before as I was not asked to and I felt it was not my place to. I asked her how she had found out, as Joe had indicated that Elvis would tell her about the decision when he came to visit his dad. She said that when Al was told the news, he asked if he could come in and tell her, which he did. He had called and said that he wanted to take her to supper. It was then that he had told that her employment with Elvis had fallen through. Her question over and over again was, "But why?" All I could do was reiterate what Joe had told me. I told her that I knew that this was a terrible blow, but that perhaps one day she could look back and see that this was the best thing that could have happened to her although she couldn't see it at the time. She said then that Al had told her at supper that he had not wanted her to take the job to begin with.

Her big question was, "What am I going to tell people? I will be so embarrassed."

I told her that she should not be embarrassed and that she could truthfully say, "This was just not the thing for me to do. Eventually I want to go back to school, and, also people might think Elvis is sick if he has a nurse in permanent attendance." She asked what she should do about the money he had given her to spend on clothes, and I told her to enjoy them, for I felt certain that he would not expect her to return the money. The thing that concerned her the most was the humiliation after telling everyone about her new job. I reminded her that her friends would understand and the others were not important. She really seemed to be okay by then and, once she was able to compose herself, she was fine. She went back out to the floor, and I went back to Mother's room.

Around 9:30, there was a bustle of activity on the floor, and several people walked past Mother's closed door going to the suite. I knew that Elvis had arrived on the floor to see his dad, and a short while later, as I started out of our room to get ice water, the 3-11 nurse was coming down the hall with a pitcher of ice water for Elvis. She was in and out of the room quickly, and when she caught up with me she said that she was so mad at him that she felt like pouring the water all over him. Then she laughed. I told her that maybe one day she would thank him. (Two months later she admitted that it was the best thing that could have happened to her, as she was going back to school.)

About an hour later, the door to the suite opened and Elvis was standing in the doorway to Mother's room. I went to the door, and he gave me a big bear hug and said, "Here's my favorite nurse!" As you may well imagine, that made my mother's day! He came into the room and sat down on the foot of her bed for about fifteen minutes. He was sweet and gracious to her, and she, of course, was beaming. He stroked the Afghan on the foot of her bed and told her how beautiful it was. She told him that I had had it made for her for Christmas a year before, as a gift from Catherine and me, and he said, "She never put anything like that on my bed."

Mother was discharged from the hospital the following day, and I'm sure that she could hardly wait to see all of her bridge buddies and church group to tell them about seeing Elvis.

Approximately another week went by before I saw Elvis again, but first I forgot to say something else about the 3-11 nurse. The day after she learned she would not be leaving on her new job, we gave her a party anyway. We had ordered the cake and had her gift, so we told her we went ahead with the surprise party because we were happy that she was not leaving us. She cried as did several of us.

About a week after this, Vernon was discharged from the hospital, and Elvis came to take him home. He arrived on the floor around 1 p.m., and I saw him coming down the hall. Everyone was really aflutter! I rounded the corner of the nurses' station and extended my hand to shake hands with him, but he brushed aside my hand and gave me a tremendous bear hug and a kiss on the cheek. We spoke a word or two, and he went on down the hall. As I went back into the nurses' station, JoAnn Berlenski, my transcriber, exclaimed, "Mrs. Cocke, how can you stay on your feet after a hug like that?" I said, "JoAnn, I'm used to it now, honey!"

Elvis had gone to his dad's room, and in just a few minutes I got a call asking me to come down to the room. When I got there, he wanted to speak to me in private so we went over into the sitting room. Elvis was concerned about the other nurse's attitude toward him the night before, and he felt that he wanted to explain his actions to me. He said that, when he asked her about going to work for him, he did not know that she was dating Al and had not been aware of it until the day Joe called me. He felt that as she was dating a member of his staff, who also traveled with him, it was not in her best interest that she take the job. Also, it was not in his best interest, for the public might think he was sick and needed constant medical attention; and, as he had Dr. Nick, who also frequently traveled with him, he realized that he had made an error in judgment by offering the job to her. He appeared genuinely sorry about the entire episode, and I told him the same things I previously had said to her. He responded that I was a wise lady and that he had come to depend on me to be his "listening post."

This morning as I write, Elvis has been gone for two months. On the way to church this morning, many thoughts about him passed through my mind. Two stand out in particular. The first was his ability to treat people as being important to him. One day I was sitting on the foot of his bed, and we were having one of our regular daily "visits." He was telling me about the day his mother died and the circumstances leading up to her death when Lamar Fike, one of the fellows who worked for him, came in. I was not overly fond of Lamar at the time; he was okay, but I thought he seemed to feel "important." At least, that was how he struck me. In later months I told Elvis about my feeling, and he said that Lamar had to be taken down a peg or two every once in a while but that he was basically okay. The longer I knew Lamar, the better I grew to like him, and he was always very pleasant.

When Lamar entered the room that day, he came in without knocking and was holding a sheaf of papers. He interrupted our conversation by saying, "Boss, we have some business to discuss." Elvis told him that we were talking, and that when he was ready to discuss business he would send for him. I think that was the only time I ever saw Elvis "pull rank."

Once Elvis told me how he had met some of the fellows who worked for him. He had been stationed in Texas, I think, when his mother went into the hospital that last time. He had great difficulty getting a leave, and told me that he finally went to the captain of his outfit and said, "Sir, I *respectfully* request an emergency leave to go home and see about my mother, or I'm going AWOL if I have to in order to see her." The captain agreed that he could go home, and he left immediately. After he arrived in Memphis he went to the hospital and visited his mother, and when he kissed her goodnight and started out the door, she said to him, "Son, when you get here tomorrow I want you to see that all these flowers are given to other patients." He told me that these were the last words she ever spoke to him.

After he went home and to bed, he said the phone rang somewhere around 3:00 a.m., and he knew immediately that his mother was gone. Emotion filled his voice as he spoke to me about that period of time. He told me about her funeral and having to leave soon afterward for Germany. On the troopship he was besieged for autographs until his company commander finally requested that he be given a small stateroom so he would not be constantly bothered by well-meaning GIs. This was done. Charlie Hodge, also a Southern boy, was moved in with him to keep him company. He and Charlie remained good friends through all those years and up to the last. Elvis also told me how he met Joe and Lamar, but Charlie was the one he spoke about the most.

The other thing that stood out in my mind was the genuine kindness and concern this man had for people. He always treated me with the utmost courtesy and respect, and the guys followed suit because they too were courteous. Elvis told me one day that I was one of the few people he knew who never asked anything of him except friendship. That "gift" from him was a treasure I have held on to the most, especially when I really "get down" and miss him so much.

That day that Elvis took his dad home was the last I was to see of him for five months. When they left, he put his arm around me and kissed me on the cheek and said that "someday" he was going to have me out to Graceland for a visit.

3.   Elvis On My Floor Again

$\mathcal{T}$hat day in March when Elvis came to take his dad home from the hospital was the last time I would see him for about five months. He went on to Los Angeles, made a trip to Hawaii, and just caught up on his rest in general. When Dr. Nick would come by the floor where I worked, he would always tell that Elvis had asked about me. Al Strada was a patient on my floor during this five-month period of time, having been in an auto accident, and George Klein was also a patient. George's wife Barbara called me at home and asked me to get him on my unit, and Al, who had been taken to the Methodist hospital, called from there to say that he had been injured and to ask if I could get him a room on my floor. He said if I could, he would have his physician discharge him from Methodist and he would come to Baptist, which is what he did. These two boys both said that Elvis had wanted them to come to my floor because he knew they would have good care.

Elvis always told me, not only with his first hospitalization but also the others to come, that he got better care when I was on duty, and he always missed me when I was off. Further along in my story, I will relate how that was solved.

The days, weeks, and months went by. It is difficult to say how this young man had touched my life. I could always tell when he was out of town (even before I was told that he was away) because the city seemed dull and the atmosphere seemed blah.

One day in August I was driving home from work

and I thought, "Gee, I'd like to see Elvis again." I came on home, cooked dinner, watched television for awhile, and went to bed. The following morning I received a call: "Elvis wants you to get his rooms ready; he came off stage in Las Vegas last night and said, 'Call Mrs. Cocke.'" I asked what was wrong with him and was told that he was sick and was coming home. He wanted me to know that he was coming in so I could get ready for him.

There was a patient in the suite who had been there for a couple of weeks. He and his wife were extremely nice, and I called Maurice Elliott, the vice-president of the hospital, and told him what was going on. He gave me an okay to ask this man if he would be willing to move to another suite. I met the wife in the hall and explained to her what was going on, and she said, "Absolutely not!" I told her that there was an available suite on 16ME which was identical to the one they had, even nicer, as it was carpeted, and I asked if she would let me speak to her husband and then show her the suite on 16ME. She agreed, and I said a silent prayer as I walked down the hall with her. When we went in the suite and talked to the patient, he couldn't have been more gracious. I took his wife down to 16ME so she could see the other suite, and she was pleased; she said she would agree willingly as her husband was agreeable. The hospital transferred their belongings and sent them a huge fruit basket with a note of thanks, and after Elvis came in and I told him all this, he sent flowers to them.

Around 9:30 a.m. the floor secretary told me I had a call. It was Elvis. He was home, would check in around midnight, and would I please meet him at the hospital that night? I assured Elvis that I would meet him that night around midnight and that as soon as we completed the transfer for the other patient, we would get the room ready for him. He laughed and said, "Mrs. Cocke, I can see you now. You'd get that man out of that room if you had to drag him out." He also said, "If there are any problems, I will wait on the suite, but I won't go to anyone else's floor." I assured him there were no problems, that the man was very gracious.

I got off work at 3 p.m., came home to cook dinner for my family, and to get my clothes together for the next day at work as I didn't want to go in uniform to the hospital that night. When Katey came home from work and found out what was going on, she was excited that Elvis would be on my unit once again.

Following dinner that night, I stretched out on the couch in the den to watch TV and cat nap until time to head back to the hospital. Around 11:00 one of the boys called to say they were about ready to leave Graceland, so I left home then.

When I got to the hospital, believe it or not, the air was filled with static electricity, and I knew that he was already there! When I got up on the floor, there were a number of guards about, so I knew that my premonition that he was already there was a reality. I went to my office and put my uniform and coat up and headed for the suite. The door was guarded by two hospital

37

guards and one of the fellows who worked for Elvis. Even at that time of night people were coming to the floor, and patients were coming out in the hall. I went into the suite; Dr. Nick was there along with Vernon (Elvis' dad), Al Strada, Dick Grob, Joe Esposito, and Dean Nichopolus. On the bed sat Elvis with his usual big grin on his face. I spoke to each one in the room as I made my way to the bed where I got the big "Elvis Presley special bear hug." I was pleased to see that he really looked quite well, although he did appear to be tired. Linda Thompson came in about that time, and I was pleased to see her. In the past we had gotten along quite well, and I was fond of her. As soon as I arrived in the room and had an opportunity to speak to everyone, all of them, with the exception of Linda and Dean, left.

Elvis went into the bathroom to change into his pajamas and to get a robe, and I went into the sitting room with Dean and Linda. He came in within a few minutes and stood by the windows. He walked over, put his arm around my shoulders and said, "You know, Mrs. Cocke, I feel better already!" He said he knew, once he got home, that I would see to it that he was taken care of, and that when he had left the stage in Las Vegas the previous night, he had told Dean to get me on the phone. He turned, started across the room, snapped his fingers as he turned back to me, and said, "By the way, I have a white 1976 Cadillac, I mean Grand Prix, coming for you tomorrow." I was so completely astounded that I just stood there in shock, looking at him. He laughed and said, "Mrs. Cocke, I've been thinking for sometime about a new car for you, and when I knew I was coming home, I knew that I wanted you to have your car."

He went on to say that he wanted to give me a car that he knew I could afford to operate, and that was why he was giving me a Grand Prix instead of a Cadillac. I told him that I appreciated his wanting to do that for me, but that I really didn't need a car. He asked me what kind of car I had, and I told him I had a 1971 Ford Galaxy. He replied, "Hell, Mrs. Cocke, you're going to have a new car whether you want it or not." Of course, I was not only speechless, but also thrilled and excited. Elvis laughed and said he had never thought he would see me when I couldn't talk. He planned to have my car delivered by noon the next day, but said if I wanted it then, he would have Dean call the man to bring it on over to me. By then, it was 2 a.m., so I said no, I might not be able to work the next day!

We sat in the suite and talked all night long. Elvis asked me if I was going to sell my car (the Ford), and I told him that I had a sister, Catherine Vonder Hoya, who lived in Dallas and who could use a good car, and I thought I'd give it to her.

When I went out on the floor to go to work around 6:30 a.m., I didn't say a word to a soul about the car that was to be delivered. The morning was pretty busy. We had a lot of sick folks on the floor, and I was really "ginning around" being about my Father's work. Around 9:00 a.m., Maurice Elliott came up on the floor to see if everything had gone off smoothly, and I asked to speak to him in private. We went into the west utility room, and I told him about the car that was to arrive at 12 noon. I explained what I had said to Elvis about not needing the car; that although I was excited, I in no way wanted to embarrass the hospital, and should I accept it? He responded that by all means I should take the car. He was as pleased and excited as I was.

After I had hospital approval, I then called Bob at home, Katey at work, and my mother to tell them about the car, but I asked that they not say anything to anyone other than for Mother to call Daddy in Mississippi (he was visiting Dick) and Patty at work. Everyone was so tickled! I still had not told the floor personnel. Around 11:30 or so, Elvis called me down to his room. He was hungry and asked would I order him some breakfast. I called dietary and ordered him fresh strawberries, bacon and eggs, toast, and coffee. While he went in to bathe and shave, I went to the linen room for bed linens to change his bed, and as I started down the hall the lady came up from dietary with the breakfast tray. When I got to the suite with my linen supplies and tray, Elvis had gone into the sitting room, so I took his tray in to him. Linda was there, as was Dean, and they were having coffee. I told them that I would be in the bedroom making the bed, so I went about my business.

I was about halfway through making the bed when Elvis came to the door and asked me to come across the hall to the sitting room. By the time I got in there, he was over at the window looking out, as were Dean and Linda. He told me to come over, and when I did, he

40

pointed out my beautiful white Grand Prix and handed me the keys. I started to cry, and he put his arm around me and said, "Bless your heart. Go drive that new car."

I flew out of that room, stopped at the nurses' station to tell the girls where I was going, and called Janet Stroud to ask her to get Miss Farnell and Sally Jo Nethery, one of the assistant directors, and they should meet me in the Madison East lobby. They were there when I got downstairs, and the four of us crossed Madison to get to my car, parked in front of the new medical building. I turned and looked up toward the suite and, although the suite was on the 18th floor, I could see the smile on that boy's face. The man who had delivered the car, told me to drive around the circle drive because he knew Elvis wanted to see me drive the car; I got in, drove around the circle, and ran over the curb! When I looked toward the suite window, I could see his hand over his eyes. Janet and Sally Jo got in the back seat and Miss Farnell got in the front, and I drove over to the parking lot to put my car in the garage and get back to work.

Let me describe my car: white on white, leather upholstery, maroon carpeting, and maroon leather dashboard; it is purely beautiful and fully equipped.

After parking the car, we went back to the hospital, this time having to cross over Union Avenue. The others went to the nursing office, and I went to the floor. Let me stop here and say that after I had told Maurice Elliott about the car, I had told Miss Farnell and Janet, and they also had thought it great and were pleased for me. I went to Elvis' room; that big grin and another bear hug awaited me. He was as happy as I was. You just cannot know how happy this day was!

Reflection — I forgot to say that before my car arrived that day, WMC-TV had come over, and I had been interviewed outside the suite. I didn't tell them that I was getting a car. I think I still thought that it was a dream, and I was afraid to say anything.

Would you believe that after I left his room and went back to work, I was actually able to work? Oh, I was excited, and each room I went in they knew about my car, and the patients were so happy for me, too. I won't say that everybody in the building was overjoyed, for the green-eyed monster reared its ugly head more than once in the next few days. There even was some criticism of the administrators for allowing me to accept the car.

When I was ready to leave the hospital that afternoon, Elvis asked me to come to his room before I left. He told me to call him when I got home to let him know I had arrived safely after running over the curb earlier.

I had called all the family right after I got the car so they could tell anyone they wanted to. Katey works at Helen of Memphis, an exclusive ladies' shop, so all there knew about it, and Mother really had a heyday calling her friends.

As I left Elvis' room and got back to the nurses' station, there was a note for me to stop by Maurice Elliot's office as I left. When I got there, he had called a photographer from *The Commercial Appeal* and wanted my picture in the paper so would I please get my car and drive over to the Union entrance of the hospital. By the time I got to the garage and back with the car, not only was there a photographer there, but also TV cameras from all three television stations in town. I was asked to get out of the car, walk around it, open the door, etc., and the cameras "rolled." I felt like I had two heads. I had seen a good friend, Virginia Morehead, coming out of the building and had waved her over to be with me, as I was embarrassed, but she wouldn't come. I remember saying, "Glory, I feel like a nut." When this film was shown on TV, part of that sentence could be heard, and the announcer laughed as he went on to talk about my car. I was really on TV that night, all three channels, and the talk of the town!

When I got home, Bob was waiting out in the driveway for me and eager to take a spin. I handed him the keys and came into the house to call Elvis. He was glad I had made it home and told me that the next time he gave me a car, he would make sure that I had finished making his bed. Who made it? He laughed and said he had.

As soon as I talked to him, I called Mother so she could watch the news. Then I called Daddy in Waynesboro, Mississippi, and Catherine in Dallas and told her that if she, Sally, and John would fly to Memphis, I'd give her the Ford. She was as flabbergasted over her car as I had been over my Grand Prix. Our phone continued to ring the rest of the afternoon, and a photographer from *The Press Scimitar* came out to make pictures. I then fixed dinner. Katey got home, and she too wanted to drive the car.

After dinner, Elvis called to ask me to come back to the hospital, and a pattern was established that was to last for several months. First, however, after we had dinner, Bob, Katey, and I drove to town in the new car, went by the Belvedere so Mother and Patty could see it, and then we went on to the hospital so Bob and Katey could take the Ford home.

Now, to backtrack a little. The night that Elvis had come in (the preceding evening), he had asked me if my family would object to me staying at the hospital at night as he always felt more secure with me there. I had discussed this with Bob and Katey, and they had agreed. In fact, Katey was thrilled beyond words that her mother was taking care of Elvis Presley. Each night, I would come home, fix dinner, eat with my family, visit a while, then go back to the hospital, taking my uniform with me for the next day. I had a room right outside the suite, and I stayed every night, usually getting back to the hospital around 9 p.m.

When I got back to the suite, after Bob and Katey drove the Ford home, Elvis was watching TV. He said, "Well, Mrs. Cocke, you're really making the news; you are a celebrity." He was really tickled that I had been so in the limelight, and we sat and rehashed the events of the previous night and that day. I told him that I had called my sister and that she and her children were flying in early the next morning to get the Ford.

Elvis and I sat up most of that night talking. Around 4 a.m. I went to my room for a few hours' sleep. I was off that weekend, so I didn't have to get up early. Yet from force of habit I did awaken in a couple of hours, checked on him in his room and found him sleeping, let the floor nurses know that I was leaving, and went home. The nurse in charge of each shift was to have sole responsibility for taking care of Elvis, and I gave their respective names to the guard before I left.

I got home around 7:30 or 8:00. Bob and Katey were both up and said the phone had been ringing since daybreak. The paper had put my picture and the car on the front page, and there was a big write-up. The phone continued to ring; I imagine that we had in excess of two hundred calls. Many were just to say "Congratulations," but some asked for my old car. One lady asked me if I would get Elvis to buy her a four-door car as she took "old folks" to the grocery, doctor, etc., and it was very difficult in her two-door car for them to get in the back seat; because she was "so good" to haul these folks around, she felt that she also deserved a car. I was furious, but did remember that I not only represented myself, but also the institution where I worked and Elvis, so I kept my cool; I did suggest that she "haul the poor old souls" around in a cab as it had four doors.

I received many fine calls, but the greatest was from a girl who had been my roommate in nursing school during our last year and a half there. Barbara Morton Bowman had seen me on TV and in the paper. She lived right here in Memphis and had for twelve years with neither of us knowing the other was here. It was six months before I was to see her, but we talked several times on the phone.

My sister, along with Sally and John, had gotten to town early and called, and Patty was to bring them out to the house in mid-afternoon. When they got here, Bob had taken the car (Ford) up to have it cleaned and filled with gas; within the past three months we had bought five new radial tires and a new battery for it, so it was really in good shape. They were as pleased with their "new car" as I was with mine, and we went for a ride in mine so Catherine and Sally could drive it. Sally told me that she had been at work when her mother called her and told her about my car, and she had been very excited telling everyone. Sally went to Eastfield Junior College and worked for Coca Cola every afternoon, and she, like all kids her age, was beside herself.

Daddy was not at home when I got my car. As I wrote earlier, he was in Waynesboro, Mississippi, visiting my brother Dick and his family. I called them late Friday afternoon, and Mother had already called them; they were all sitting around the kitchen table having coffee and talking about my car. Susan and Jill, Dick's two girls, were as excited as Katey, Sally, and John had been.

After Catherine, Patty, Sal, and John left, we tried to settle down at home and get a little rest, which, with the frequent phone calls, was hard to do. I fixed our dinner around 6:30; then, around 8:30 or 9:00, I was on my way back to the hospital.

46

Elvis was in his room alone watching TV. Several of the fellows who worked for him were in the sitting room watching TV, as was Linda. I went into his room, his face lit up in a big smile, and he said he was glad I was back because he had missed me. He many times reminded me that he felt better when I was around, and he knew he could depend on me. I was his security blanket, and he didn't hesitate to say so.

During this hospital stay, Margaret Rich was admitted to the hospital and was a patient on my floor. She is the wife of Charlie Rich. Although I did not see him, she was really a nice girl. He wanted her to have a suite, but the only one available on my floor was occupied, so she moved down to 16 Madison East. I really hated to see her leave because she was so pleasant. She came back up to the floor many days later bringing a tray of cheese to Elvis, but he had gone home the night before. When I told him about it, he was really very appreciative of her doing such a nice thing and said that he liked both her and Charlie

We spent every night for weeks following this same pattern I have just mentioned. If I was off duty (my days off), I still stayed at the hospital at night, coming back around 9 p.m., and returning home the next morning. If I had to work, I got up and was already at work. Elvis had a regular patient room for me right outside the suite where the guard was, so I had my bathroom, phone, TV, etc., and usually kept extra clothes and uniforms there just as I did at home. My room was blocked off from the rest of the floor, as was the entire suite area. I had many offers from people wanting to "help me out" with my extra duties. Here again, that old green-eyed monster reared its ugly head. All of my actions—staying the night at the hospital, etc.—had administration approval.

Actually, it was comical that there were individuals who would get out and let the world know how tacky they could be by being disgruntled over another's stroke of luck. One of the pharmacists was highly critical about my car, and I told him that if I was so "little" as to be catty about someone's good luck, I would at least be smart enough to keep my mouth shut and not let people know I could be so tacky. To my knowledge, he never had another word to say. We are good friends and respect each other, so the car did not dissolve a friendship.

One day when I was off duty, Bob and I drove down to Hudsonville, a little community out from Holly Springs, Mississippi. We wanted to show his aunt, Mary Lewis Cocke, the car. Irene, one of the black ladies who lives on the farm, came into Mary Lewis' country store and when I took her out to see the car, she said, "Oh, Miss Marian, is this the car that Elvis Precious gave you?" She always referred to him that way, and after he died, she hugged me and cried and said that there would never be another Elvis Precious.

Elvis and I really had great conversations during this period of time. He was most considerate of the fact that fives times a week I had to get up early in the morning and go to work. On those days, I went to bed by 11:00

p.m.; the days I didn't have to get up with the chickens to go to work, we would most likely sit up all night and talk. We talked about our families, his child, and mine — the things that good friends sit up and talk about. There was never a night he didn't mention his mother and usually his dad. He called him "Daddy."

Through the entire period of time I was associated with this boy, the thing that stood out the most to me was his love for his family. He told me one night that he really depended on them, that they never had let him down, and that he had tried never to let them down. Once one family member heard someone say Elvis really liked others around him in preference to them. This was not so, else why did he have them so close by him, even living in the same house with him. He wanted them with him. He spoke with great love for these people; he told me again about the events leading to his mother's death, his going to Germany, and having his dad and grandmother fly over (he called Grandma "Dodger"), how he met Priscilla, and about their courtship. I think that I have never heard any man speak so lovingly about a woman. He had many beautiful things to say about her, and any conversation we had about her most often wound up with, "You know, Mrs. Cocke, I'll always love Priscilla." Lisa, his daughter, was a favorite subject. How he loved that little girl! She was really the bright star in his life, and he admitted that he found it very hard to discipline her, but that he tried to be a good daddy. He bragged about Priscilla as a wife and mother and always said she was a very special person.

So went my days and nights. Our talks mainly were family oriented, but many times we also talked about astrology and history. Elvis was a well-read young man and had an excellent mind. For example, one day Dr. Nick came up on the floor and brought Father Vierons, the Greek priest, with him. Dr. Nick later laughed and said that Father Vierons was amazed at Elvis' knowledge of the Bible. Elvis liked Father Vierons and said later that he had really enjoyed his visit with him.

Many flowers, letters, and cards arrived by the truckload daily and were put in the room across the hall from my room. I would select a fresh vase of flowers every day to take into the suite, and Babe would come out every afternoon late, look at the flowers and baskets of fruit, and then ask us to have the flowers taken to patients throughout the hospital, particularly to the old, the young, and the very ill.

One day, as he started out of the suite door, Carolyn Pulliam, Dr. Groner's secretary, had come up to see me for a few minutes and I had taken her to the flower room to see the flowers. As Elvis got to the door of the suite, Carolyn started out the other door, and she ducked back into the room. I called to her and she came out. I introduced her to Elvis. Carolyn is a beautiful lady with prematurely gray hair, but the nicest thing you can say about her is that she has an inner beauty that outshines her exterior beauty. In that brief moment that they met, Elvis recognized this quality in her, and he later commented that he knew that she was a Christian because she glowed with her love for the Lord.

Elvis was an extremely religious man. He didn't like to be referred to as a "super-star," and he had mixed feelings about being referred to as the "King." He said that to be referred to as "the king of rock and roll," or some such title, was okay, he guessed, but he added — with tears in his eyes — "There is only one King, and that is Christ."

While Elvis was in the hospital this time, many things were asked of me. One day a little runner from X-ray came up and said that she didn't want anything for herself, but that she had an aunt who needed financial aid and would I ask Elvis to help. I said no, I was sorry, but I couldn't do that. She turned around and left — and never spoke to me again.

Another day a lady who worked in a physician's office at the University of Tennessee Medical Center came to the floor and asked for me. She said that her boss had told her to come see me, as he knew that I could get her in to see Elvis so that she might might ask for help. Once again I said no, I'm sorry.

I received many letters after Elvis gave me my car. Many expressed happiness for me, but many asked for money from the boy — as much as ten to fifteen thousand dollars. The funds were "to set me up in business" or "just a loan." One man wanted to get a loan from a bank to open a photography studio, and he felt that if he could go out to Graceland and make shots of Elvis' house, the bank would see how good he was and he could get his loan. Others wanted money for anything from repairing nursing homes to opening a garage.

Many letters also came to thank me for taking care of Elvis, and these restored my faith in people. I never mentioned the requests for money to Elvis, but I made it a point to take the letters and cards to the suite when they expressed concern about his welfare. He was so appreciative of all the gifts and so grateful to the people who wrote.

One letter I received was particularly funny. It was from Johannesburg, South Africa. The person who wrote was coming to this country to go to school, and she had seen the picture in the paper of me and my car. She wrote that she needed an automobile in order to "motor" to and from school, and would I please pass the word on to Elvis so there would be a car waiting for her upon her arrival in this country. She also said for me to thank him in advance.

I also had requests for a lock of his hair, for his tooth-brush, for his comb, even for some of his blood!

Reflections about these three weeks: Great! I had spent many hours just visiting with Elvis. And I had come to know each of the boys who worked for him a little better. I had my favorites, but got along well with each of them.

Red and Sonny West, who were cousins, were always polite and nice. Sonny was friendlier, but I liked them both equally. Al Strada was there often, as were Dean, Dick, Jerry, David Leech, and Billy Smith. Billy Smith was Elvis' cousin and a tremendous favorite with Elvis; I think Elvis trusted him more than any of all the boys. David Leech and Al Strada were my favorites. Al told me that he had been a medical student when he went to work for Elvis and that he owed a lot of money at the time. He said Elvis had paid his bills and had always been very good to him. Al is still at Graceland. He is a good and very sincere person.

I really liked all the boys — with the exception of Dave Hebler, but I do have to be honest and say that he was always polite and friendly. One thing I can certainly say: they were all different. Al and David were both cute boys and would come in and help me make Elvis' bed a lot of times. They also would go out to the dietary and get ice water or juice for him or go across the street to the Steak and Egg and get him a bacon-burger if he got hungry during the night.

Little did I realize while Elvis was in the hospital during this stay how well I would get to know all these boys in the days and weeks to come.

4. Graceland

*a*fter Elvis had been in the hospital about two and a half weeks, his doctors decided he was about ready for discharge. He had been admitted for a colon problem, as well as for being tired. He was rested, and medication had eased his colon troubles. Moreover, he could continue on medication for his colon while at home. Dr. Nick asked Elvis if he wanted to get private nurses to go to Graceland to keep him on his medical schedule. Elvis said no, he wanted Mrs. Cocke to go with him and keep the same schedule we had in the hospital!

I was pleased and flattered that he wanted me to go to Graceland and replied that I would talk it over with my family. Elvis was always considerate and wanted me to have my husband's approval. He and Dr. Nick also felt it would be nice to have someone else at Graceland during a few hours of the day, so the 3-11 p.m. nurse, who had been on hand during this hospitalization, was asked to come to Graceland every day from 9 a.m. until 2 p.m.; then she would come on to work at 3 p.m. at the hospital. Her name was Kathy Seamon, and she was an awfully sweet girl who was married to a navy man stationed at the base in Millington.

Kathy and I were both pleased about our "special pleasure" — it couldn't be called a job! We both spoke to our husbands and got their approval. Our only stipulation about going to Graceland to care for Elvis was that neither of us, in any way, wanted to be paid for what we did for him; we wanted our time to be a gift to him because he had always given so much to others.

The night before we were to go to Graceland, Elvis, Jerry Schilling, Dick Grob, and I were in the suite sitting room. We were talking about our move the next night as to time, etc. Elvis had just autographed a picture of himself which said, "To Mrs. Cocke, the sex symbol of the Babtist" (his spelling of Baptist)! Jerry made a wisecrack about mine and Kathy's last names. I reached over on the bedside table, picked up a full pitcher of ice water (more ice than water), walked over to Jerry, pulled the neck of his shirt out, and poured the entire contents of the pitcher down his shirt; it happened so quickly he didn't realize what was going on. Elvis laughed until he cried and said I was going to work out just great at Graceland. He also suggested to Jerry that he watch himself. Jerry took his "dousing" in stride, and we all laughed about it.

The night of hospital departure was upon us, and we tried hard to "keep the lid on" so we would not be mobbed when we left the building. Linda T. was there, so was Dick Grob, Dean, and Al. We decided that we would leave the suite and go up the stairway to the 19th floor, which had not yet been opened for patients. There we would get on the service elevator, go to the first floor, through dietary, and out the back door where we would go in my car. I was extremely pleased to be using my car, and I asked Dick Grob to drive.

I picked up the medications we were to take to Graceland with us then, for Kathy was the only one who knew we were leaving. I signed off the ward chart and gave it to Kathy to lock up until I came back to work on Monday morning.

Elvis, Dick, Linda, and I, escorted by hospital security, departed as we had planned, leaving Dean and Al Strada behind to take care of getting the clothes and other personal property — radio, stereo, and records, etc. — removed to Graceland.

The date was September 5, 1975. We left the Baptist Hospital around 9:30 p.m. Dick was driving, with Elvis in the front seat by him, while Linda and I sat in the back. Elvis lit a cigar, and when he put it out just before we got to Graceland, he put it in the ashtray. I still have that butt sealed up in a small plastic bag. I told Elvis about this sometime later, and he patted my hand and said, "Did you really? Mrs. Cocke, you're really something!"

As we approached the gates of Graceland, you could see a crowd of people gathered. They didn't know he was coming home; as on any other night, there were fans there all the time, even when he was out of town. The fans still come to Graceland.

We drove through the gates with everyone making a rush for the car. The light was on on the front porch, and he told me that when he was out of town the light was always off. We went into the foyer and he turned, stretched his arms wide, and said, "Be it ever so humble, there's no place like home." He told me to come on upstairs, and after he put my bag down (he carried it up the stairs for me), he showed me the upstairs: his study, bedroom, bath, and dressing room. All were quietly elegant with the exception of the TV sets; there were two in the ceiling over the king-size bed, a small one on the table beside the bed, and a large console at the foot. There also was one in the bathroom. The study was particularly handsome, but the thing that impressed me the most was that all the rooms were comfortable and looked lived in; it was obvious that this home was enjoyed and not just a house. There was a large poster-size picture of a blown up snapshot that stood by the console TV. It was of him and his mother. He was two or three years old and wore overalls and a hat. He was a cute little fella! Lisa's room had, or has, a round carousel king-size bed in white imitation fur. There was a day bed, a chair, a small built-in refrigerator, a small TV, and a bathroom; all of her furnishings and decor were in gold and white.

Elvis told me that I should sleep on the big bed because he wanted me to be comfortable, and he told Dick that he wanted a larger TV set brought in for me. Linda then took me on a tour of the house. Throughout our tour I felt the warmth of home present. The living room and music room had red and white furniture, drapes, and carpet, but it was certainly not garish or "fire engine red." It was a room that I was to sit and relax in many times with Delta; usually I kicked my shoes off and tucked my feet up under me just as I do at home. The dining room has a very large oval table with a mirrored top; the chairs are deep red, King Arthur type, and there are beautiful mirrors and china cabinets in the room. The kitchen is a warm family room. The lower level had the game room and a TV-type room; the laundry room was also in the lower level, as was Charlie Hodge's room and bath. I have read many times that there is a "huge ballroom" at Graceland. Not so; there is not even a "small ballroom."

After my tour of the house, Linda and I went back upstairs to Elvis' room. He had put on a pair of pajamas and was sitting in the bed watching TV. It was about time for his medicine (I had put it in Lisa's room), so I went for that, got him a glass of water, and got him "settled for the night." He was really feeling great, and he looked good. He asked me if I was tired, and I said yes, I was both tired and hungry, and I wanted a bowl of cereal. He told me then that I was "at home," and anything I wanted was at my disposal. Linda went back to Lisa's room, showed me the local numbers to call for the kitchen, Delta, Grandma, etc., and Elvis' local number. She asked what I wanted to eat, then called the kitchen and asked that a bowl of cereal be brought up for me. While I was waiting for that, I readied myself for bed. In just a short time there was a knock on the door and a large black lady was standing there with a smile on her face and a tray in her hands. She told me that her name was Pauline, and if I wanted anything else I should ring for it. She had brought me a bowl of cornflakes a glass of milk, and a peeled and sliced banana on the side. I thanked her, she left, and I really devoured those cornflakes and that banana.

I went on to bed after I finished my cereal and went to sleep right away. Around 3 a.m. there was a knock on the door, and as the door was opening, I heard Elvis very quietly say, "Mrs. Cocke?" I got up, reaching for my robe, and asked if he was okay. He said that he couldn't sleep and had I brought any sleeping pills home with me. I got one out for him, which he took. He apologized for waking me and went back to bed. I got back in bed and went back to sleep immediately, not waking again until around 7 a.m., which was late sleeping for me as I am an early riser. I bathed and dressed, went down the hall to his suite to check and see if he was asleep, then went on downstairs, saw Delta and had a cup of coffee with her, went to Grandma's room and said good morning to her, and met Mary and Nancy, two of the cooks. Then I went on home to call Kathy to let her know where I had put everything and asked her to be out at the house by 10:00 a.m. I came on home, fixed breakfast for my family, and told them all about Graceland. Then I called my mother and filled her in as to what the house now looked like.

Let me regress here and say this about the house. Graceland, before Elvis bought it, was owned by Mrs. Ruth Brown Moore, a widow. This home had been in her family for many years and was named "Graceland" for her aunt. In magazines you may read that it was named for Elvis' mother, but this is not so. Mrs. Moore was a close friend of my mother's, and as Mother and Daddy had been there many times when Mrs. Moore owned the place, they were curious to know about changes. I too had been in Graceland a couple of times before Mrs. Moore sold it, and although Elvis had made many changes, the basic beauty of the home was still there.

My phone continued to ring, friends wanting to know "all about Elvis." I told one and all that he was truly a nice person. Never at any time would I answer personal questions about him, even if I knew the answers, as I felt the questions about his personal life were in poor taste. I still feel that way. People soon learned that I would not answer questions that I felt were in poor taste or just plain none of their business, and they soon stopped asking.

When I got back to Graceland that Saturday night, I went immediately to Lisa's room, read Kathy's notes, and then went to Elvis' suite. He was up and dressed after sleeping most of the day. He felt fine, and his daddy had come over to visit with him. I told him I would like to go down and visit with Delta and Grandma, if it was okay with him, and he could call me in Grandma's room if he wanted me for anything. After that, there was seldom a night that I didn't spend at least thirty minutes with these two ladies, and they are very good and cherished friends even now.

Delta Biggs was Elvis' aunt on his dad's side of the family. Next to his dad, Lisa, and Grandma, I think Elvis had a tremendous amount of love and devotion for her. He told me how she and her husband, Pat, had been great to him when he was a kid, the things they had given him for Christmas, and the love and attention they had shown him. When Pat died, suddenly and at the wheel of the car with Delta beside him, Elvis was the one Delta had called. He had arranged for the body to be brought to Memphis and had made all the necessary arrangements; then he had opened his heart and the doors of his home for Delta to move in. To this day she resides at Graceland; Elvis always said that he never knew how he had managed without Aunt Delta because she really took care of him and was so great. He truly loved and depended on this lady.

I also had met Grandma, and she is a doll! She is always beautifully dressed and immaculate. Elvis' grandmother on his father's side, she has long, slender fingers, and the tiny blue veins show clearly in the near-transparent skin on her hands. Delta has all of Grandma's dresses made, and she always wears a pretty apron. These two ladies are devoted to each other, and it was always such a pleasure to me to be able to visit with them each night. The thing that I noticed the most about Grandma was her hands (that's the first thing I notice about anyone). Grandma has beautiful hands, so soft and smooth.

I also came to know the rest of the family at Graceland. Nash was another aunt. She lives with her husband, Earl Pritchett, in a large trailer house on the northeast corner of the Graceland estate. Earl is the man who keeps the grounds so beautifully and sees that the appearance is always in top shape. He also does any minor and often major repairs, and is a hard-working man. Elvis told me that Aunt Nash was a minister; he used to say, "She's really a good preacher!" It was most evident that he loved her too, and had a lot of respect and friendship for Earl.

Vester is Vernon's brother, and he is always at the gate during the days of the week. The only thing that Elvis ever really said about Vester was that he liked to give interviews. But he was very fond of him.

That Saturday night some of the fellows who worked for Elvis came over to see him, so I only saw him at "pill time." One of the medications that he took for his colon problem had a particularly bad taste, and he would always "yuk" and say, "Do I have to take it?" I'd tell him, "Yes," so he would down it quickly and chase it with a lot of water. I told him what I used to tell Katey when she was a little girl: "If you spit this out, I've got lots more just like it, so swallow it!" He also took medication for hypertension. Elvis could have been given these medications by anyone on his house staff, but I think that he really enjoyed being with Kathy and with me, and he had us there for company as much as anything; Kathy was younger, but I was his security blanket; many times he reminded me of this, and said he always felt better when I was close by.

Sunday morning when I got up, I bathed and dressed and went to the suite to check on my boy. He was sitting up in his bed with the Sunday paper spread out in front of him and the large TV set on. We talked for a few minutes, and I gave him his medication, then went downstairs to have breakfast with Grandma before going to church where I met my family: Bob, Katey, Mother, Daddy, and Patty. Patty, my sister, and Katey were in the choir, but the remaining four of us always sat together.

After church we went out to eat, then we went home and so did my folks. I read the paper and we watched the ball game. During the afternoon we went for a ride, then came back home for a snack type supper. Around 6:00 the phone rang. It was Elvis wanting to know if I could possibly come out earlier, so I headed back to Graceland.

I always got a "special charge" out of being able to drive up to the gates at Graceland and being waved right on through. (Now it is different.) There was an unusually large crowd there that Sunday, as Elvis had only been home from the hospital two days. Everyone hoped to catch a glimpse of him. When I entered the house, I went immediately to the suite; because he had called and asked me to come out early, I was afraid he might not be feeling well. He was sitting in his room, and beside him was a long, slender, green velvet box. With his eyes shining and excitement in his voice, he told me that he had a gift for me; he opened the box and took out a long slender chain with an emblem that said "TLC" and had a bolt of lightning. He asked me to take off my glasses so he could put the chain over my head. As he did so, he said, "Of all the people I know, you really give me TLC, and you have certainly more than earned this."

I burst into tears, and he hugged me and said, "Bless your heart, Mrs. Cocke, don't cry. You are officially one of the gang now." Of the two previous gifts he had given me, this by far was — and still is — my most treasured material possession. He put it on me, and I have not taken it off. I wear the chain under my uniform when I'm on duty, but any other time it can be seen around my neck in full view unless I have on the cross. Then it is once again under my clothing.

Elvis and I spent many happy months together, and our nights followed the same pattern: I would get to Graceland every night around 8 p.m. and go immediately to Lisa's room. I would check in the kitchen before I went upstairs to see if he was awake. If he was, as soon as I got to Lisa's room, I would buzz his room to let him know I was there. If he had not called the kitchen to let Lottie, the night cook, know that he was awake, I would go to Lisa's room, put up my jacket and purse, and go back downstairs to sit with Grandma and Delta until he called down. Usually I was able to visit with them around thirty minutes, but sometimes I stayed an hour and sometimes I didn't get to visit with them until quite late or not at all other than just for a pop-in visit.

But to the way our nights went . . .

One of my first nights at Graceland I was sitting in Lisa's room watching television and drinking a cup of coffee. It was about 8:30. All of a sudden I heard a noise coming down the hall that sounded like a herd of elephants. The door was ajar rather than being closed all the way, and it burst open. There stood Elvis in his blue pajamas, and robe, barefooted, and holding his breakfast tray (remember that he ate breakfast at night because he was a daytime sleeper most of the time). He said, "Hell, Mrs. Cocke, I don't want to sit in there. I'd rather be in here with you." I pulled the little stool over to the chair for his tray, and he sat down to eat. I called the kitchen and asked Pauline if she or Maggie would bring us another pot of coffee, and when Pauline brought it up, she said, "Mr. P., Mr. P., you really something!" Thereafter he always ate in that room.

The first night he came in with his tray, I asked him if he would like me to "lather" his coffee. He laughed and asked what that was, and I told him it meant to add cream and sugar. He replied, "Please do." Every night thereafter he would ask me to "lather" his coffee, saying I lathered it better than he did.

One night, after he had eaten and wanted something cold to drink, I asked, "Do you want ice water or belly wash?" "What the heck is belly wash?" he wanted to know. I told him that it was his favorite soda pop. From then on, when we were ready to have a cold drink after coffee, he would specify belly wash.

One night we were having coffee, and Elvis asked me if I knew how to make banana pudding. I said sure. He asked if I would bring him some the next night because he was hungry for it. One of the cooks downstairs would have made it in a minute, but he asked me to do it, so I said okay. The next night, when I came out to Graceland, I took the pudding and went upstairs with it. As soon as I got in Lisa's room, he came in and asked, "Did you bring it?"

We put it in the refrigerator, and I called for his breakfast tray and our coffee. He ate sparingly of his breakfast, and when Maggie came for his tray, he kept his spoon. As soon as she left, just like a kid he said, "Now, get the banana pudding!" He ate it right out of the bowl in which I had brought it without me putting some into a smaller bowl. In fact, he ate half of it. The next night he ate the other half, and, believe me, that was a big banana pudding.

On another occasion I was making an Afghan for our "two girls," chihuahua dogs named Liz and Honeybunch. I usually worked on it every night as we visited, and he kept eyeing it. I had told him why I was making it, and he liked it very much. Every night after I finished working on it, he would put it over his knees if he got chilly. That Afghan is now wrapped in tissue paper and put up. I made another for the puppies.

One night he came in with a pair of white athletic socks. He put them on, and there was a hole in the heel of one, so he took it off and tossed it on the day bed. I picked it up and darned it. He watched me, and when I finished I threw it in the waste can. He laughed and asked why I had bothered to darn the socks if I was going to throw them away. I answered, "So I can say I darned Elvis Presley's socks!" He just laughed.

One night when we were talking about his making records, Elvis told me about the first one he had cut. He said that some time later he had been driving down Union Avenue in Memphis in his truck when he stopped at a red light. A man pulled up beside him, his radio playing, and Elvis' record was on. Elvis stuck his head out the window of his truck and said, "Mister, that's me singing!" As he told me this story, the pride and pleasure was still there in his voice, even after all those years, of that first record which he made for his mother's birthday.

If I did not have to work at the hospital the next day, we might sit there over many pots of coffee and talk all night long. If I had to work the next day, however, he would go back to his suite around 11:00, and Billy Smith and Linda (if she was in town) would visit him until he was ready to retire.

Elvis usually liked pretty much the same thing to eat: oatmeal, then bacon, eggs, and coffee. I asked him one night why he didn't eat his bacon and eggs first and his oatmeal last, as it would stay hot longer. He said, "Now that's why I like having you around, you think!" As everything was cold by the time he brought it to my room that first night, I asked him to let me order for him. I called the kitchen and asked that his oatmeal be put in a covered bowl and the milk be heated to pour into the cereal; the bacon and eggs were to be covered with a hot plate, and please send corn oil margarine for his oatmeal rather than butter. He sat there and watched me as I spoke to the cook, and when I hung up he said, "You're pretty smart!" When Pauline brought the fresh tray — and he had a really good meal that stayed hot while he ate it — he said, "Now why didn't they think of that!" I did ask that they not send any more butter to the room, but always the corn oil margarine. He didn't eat toast and only occasionally would like a glass of juice, so he really ate a good, well balanced meal.

We talked about many things, always family, astrology, and history, but seldom about Hollywood. We watched the Monday night football games; both of us really liked football! We would choose opposite teams, but usually would end up rooting for the same team.

Let me recall some of our visits. One night, Maggie, one of the maids, came upstairs to bring the tray with our cofeee and cups. She was "full figured," and she wore a pair of rather snug slacks. She picked up the empty coffee pot to go out, and Elvis commented to her that she was really getting broad across the butt; she grinned and walked out. I got up from the couch and, backwards, I moved over to the sink to rinse our cups with hot water. Elvis said, "Mrs. Cocke, what the hell are you doing?" and I said, "Well, I'm not going to have you telling me how wide I'm getting across the butt!" He really laughed and said, "Oh no," but seeing that twinkle in his eyes, I knew that was just exactly what he had been thinking — and he blushed.

Maggie had been hired, I think, as a maid, but she certainly had a good job. Elvis told me that the first time he ever saw her he was going in one of the Pontiac agencies and she was coming out, crying, with her mother. He grabbed her by the arm and asked her what was wrong, and she told him that she had wanted to buy a Firebird but the agency wouldn't okay her credit. He asked her if she had a job, and she told him no, that she went to school and she was looking for a part-time job. He told her to come to Graceland the next day at 5:00 p.m. to work for him; then he took her in the agency and bought her the Firebird. Her job at Graceland was to sit by the phone in the kitchen and answer it and to bring her books and study. She would occasionally take trays up to him and frequently brought coffee, but those few duties were "her job" and, to boot, I think he paid for her schooling. All of the maids really loved Elvis, called him "Mr. P.," and would have given their right arm for him anytime. Mary and Nancy were there during the day, Pauline and Lottie came in at night, and Maggie came in from 5 to 9 p.m. each night. To date, all of these ladies are still there (11/22/77).

Elvis liked karate, and he showed me many karate chops. One night he asked David Stanley, Dave Hibler, and Billy Smith to put on an exhibition for me. He also took part. I was quite impressed. Elvis was a very strong man, and he certainly excelled in this field.

Linda, Elvis, and I were all together one night in the sitting room (Lisa's room), and he was talking about astrology. It was late at night, but I was off the next day. I had on my pajamas and robe, as did he, and we referred to these times as our "pajama party." He asked me when my birthday was, but before I could tell him he asked me not to. He said that he wanted to tell me first how he felt about me. By the time he finished, which was only a couple of minutes really, the tears were in my eyes because of the beautiful things he had to say about me. When he finished, I said, "Honey, there ain't nobody that good!" Again he asked my birthday, and I told him so he did some "figuring" and thumbed through his book to see what the book had to say. The book actually was so similar to what he had said that Linda and I were both flabbergasted! We sat there with our mouths open, just amazed.

One night when I got to Graceland, Elvis was a little restless. I asked him if he wanted to go for a walk. He said, "How about a drive?" We went out the front where I tossed him the keys to my car and said, "You drive." Billy Smith was with us, and he got in the back. I sat in the front with Elvis. When we got to the gate and the fans saw Elvis at the wheel, they made a mad rush for the car. He waved at them and shouted greetings, and we drove off. When we returned to Graceland a short while later, he thanked me for letting him drive. I told him that I would not let just anyone drive my car, but that he was "sorta special."

One night, when the gang was going to a movie, I went to the kitchen to get a glass of ice water. Elvis came in right behind me and wanted water too. He went over to the sink, snapping his fingers, singing and sort of dancing as he went. Lottie, one of the cooks, asked, "Mr. P., do you know how to wiggle?"

Elvis laughed and said, "Lottie, how the hell do you think I got this big house on this hill?"

One night when Elvis and I were talking at Graceland, he commented about an article in the paper he had read. It told about Roy Clark being bothered by a fan in the lobby of a hotel, and he was rude to her, leading the woman to complain. Elvis said he understood how Roy Clark felt in that situation, commenting, "A man should be able to go out in public without being bothered." He added that he thought Roy Clark was a fine man and a great musician. This is one of the few times I heard Elvis indicate that too much attention from the fans bothered him, for he always was extremely considerate of their demands on him — which were endless when he was in public. Elvis also spoke highly of Muhammad Ali and said he was really "a good guy."

Another night, when I arrived at Graceland, it was early evening and Kathy was still there. Elvis said, "Mrs. Cocke, let's go for a ride. I've got a surprise for you and Kathy, and I asked her to wait until you got here. We're going to the airport." Kathy had called her husband to say she would be home late. We went down, piled into the limousine, and drove to the airport. I don't remember which of the fellows went with us, but Charlie Hodge came in with Maggie after we were already on the plane, and they, too, went up with us. This was the maiden voyage of the *Jet Star*, and she was a lovely plane. We circled the city, a wide sweep, and was it ever fun! Can you imagine going for a spin at night by flying around the city—and with someone like Elvis Presley!

One morning early, Elvis came in, running up the stairs and into my room. He said , "Mrs. Cocke, do you remember that doctor that came to see me when I was in the hospital, the surgeon?"

I replied, "Yes, that's John Nash."

Elvis commented with a smile, "You know, he is a hell of a nice guy, and funny too." I replied that I knew he was a nice guy but never thought about him being funny. Then Elvis told me what had happened. He had gone to play racquet ball, and John was there playing also, wearing white tennis shorts. When John got cold, he walked over and put on Elvis' coat, which came below Elvis' knees. Now that may not seem funny to anyone who doesn't know the size of these two men. Elvis was well over six feet tall, and Dr. John Nash is about 5'8".

Often as we talked, we had the TV on. If there was a football game to be seen, we watched it. Other shows were more or less incidental because mainly we just talked and drank coffee; however, he particularly enjoyed the Mary Tyler Moore show and Carol Burnett and would laugh until he cried over some of the antics of Tim Conway and Harvey Korman. After Elvis finished a meal, he would smoke a cigar, and I would have a cigarette — although I am really a non-smoker. One night as we sat talking, he suggested that we call my mother, which we did. He was such a thoughtful person, and Mother was so pleased. At the time she was recuperating from surgery, which is a separate story in itself.

5. A Fabulous Trip

n September, before Mother became ill, I called my sister in Dallas one Sunday afternoon, as I usually did, when suddenly the operator interrupted us to say that Elvis was trying to reach me. I told Catherine I would call her back and hung up. The phone rang immediately. Elvis said he was going to Dallas and wanted to know if I wanted to go. He said he was going out to see the *Lisa Marie,* his 707 private jet; he wanted to check on how it was coming along in its refurbishing process. Katey and Bob were sitting in our den, and when Katey heard my end of the conversation she put up a howl to go too. Elvis heard her and said, "Sure, bring her along." We jumped in the car and headed out after calling Mother first and asking her to let my sister Catherine know I'd call her when we reached Dallas.

When we got out to Graceland, the limo was in front of the house. Katey and I went on in, and I took her upstairs with me. She was so excited she was in tears. Elvis hugged her and told her he was glad she could come, and we headed out. What a thrill! I was accustomed to being with Elvis, but Katey wasn't, and the excitement of the crowd at the gate and her being along kept her in tears. Linda Thompson was along also, as was Dick Grob, David Stanley, Dave Hibler, and someone else, but I can't remember offhand who it was unless it was David Leech. We got out to the airport and onto the *Jet Star* and took off. Katey was still crying from happiness.

We were airborne when Elvis told me that he had bought Kathy Seamon a LeMans and given it to her that morning. I said I thought that was fantastic of him, and he told me that he didn't want to give her a car like my Grand Prix because I was special to him and to duplicate my car for her would have taken away from me. I assured him that I would not have felt that way. He said that it really made him happy to do things like that, and you could tell this was so just by looking in his eyes. He laughed and said, "But I'm not going to buy you a plane!" I told him that he had spoiled my day, and we had a good laugh.

We arrived in Fort Worth, not Dallas, about fifty minutes after leaving Memphis. A crowd had gathered at the small airport that we went to, and Elvis waved to them. We then went on board the *Lisa Marie* and made the grand tour. It was impressive although it was virtually bare of furnishings; it didn't take a lot of imagination to know that it would be a beautiful aircraft once it was properly dressed up. When we left the plane, we went to the small airport office where I called my sister in Dallas to let her know that I was in Fort Worth, but ready to leave. Then I called Bob to let him know that we would be home in an hour or so. As I hung up the phone after speaking to him, Elvis came into the office and asked me if I had ever been to Las Vegas. I told him no, so he said that we would go there too! I reminded him that I had to work the next day, and he said we would be back in time. I called Bob again and told him to look for us when he saw us coming.

When we went out to board the *Jet Star,* the crowd of fans had increased somewhat and moved closer to the plane. Elvis took time with them, gave autographs, and sent them all home happy. Immediately after leaving Fort Worth, Elvis, Linda, Katey, and I were sitting in the back of the plane talking when he reached toward his wrist and took off a gold link Gucci bracelet, leaned over, and put it on Katey's wrist, saying, "Here, sweetheart, I want you to have this." Katey burst into tears and cried most of the way to Las Vegas, a two and three-quarter hour trip. By the time we got there, she had such a headache we had to give her aspirin and coke.

As we flew over the Grand Canyon, Elvis quoted a line from the song "How Great Thou Art". "When I in Awesome Wonder." He marveled about the beauty of it as though he would never cease to be amazed by it, and there were tears in his eyes. Later, on an occasion when we were talking about his singing, I told him I loved it when he sang "How Great Thou Art." In a joking way — but I was serious — I said, "If I die before you, I want you to sing that at my funeral. But if you go first, I want a tape of you singing that song played at my funeral." "Don't you worry, Mrs. Cocke," he replied. "I'm sure I'll sing at your funeral, but if I don't, do you have a tape?" I said yes.

When we got to Las Vegas, he had Katey and me go to the front of the plane with him so we could watch the landing approach. It was really an exciting time for us. We were met at the airport by Elias Ganno, an M.D.

and close friend of Elvis', and another man, each driving separate cars. The boys went with the other man while the four of us went with Elias. He was driving his Mercedes, a gift from Elvis. We went to his home for a short visit, then Elvis told him that he wanted to go for a ride so Katey and I could see Las Vegas. We covered the strip, saw all of the big hotels, etc.—so many bright lights. Elvis then said it was time for us to leave, and he asked Elias to call the house and have the boys meet us at the airport. He commented that the plane should be gassed up and ready for departure by the time we got there. I told him if he didn't gas me up I'd never make it back to Memphis, because I was starved and knew that Katey was too. He assured me that there would be enough food for us on the plane to last us until we got home.

When we got to the airport, the boys were already there. We boarded, and there in the back of the plane were two tables spread with a sumptuous feast. There was one huge tray of fresh fruit; the other tray had roast beef and ham and cheese sandwiches, pickles, olives, celery and carrot strips, deviled eggs, fresh fruit cut up in containers, chips, dip, and cookies. There appeared to be enough to feed an army — and the boys had already eaten, as had Milo High, the pilot, and the co-pilot. We tore up that tray, going through it like a bunch of locusts; there were only crumbs left when we finished. During our meal (we were still at the airport) Elvis asked if we had ever been to Palm Springs. I told him no, so he said well we'd go there too.

I again reminded Elvis that I had to go to work the next day, and again he said he would have me home on time. He picked up the phone, called the cockpit, and told the pilot to head for Palm Springs. He then turned to me and said, "Hell Mrs. Cocke, we're almost going to fly over my house anyway, so we might as well stop."

We left for Palm Springs, arriving there in twenty or thirty minutes from Las Vegas. When we got to the airport, Dick went inside and rented a station wagon, and we all piled in and headed for the house. What a house! It was truly beautiful, exactly what you expect a man like Elvis to own. It was as elegant as Graceland, but a much "quieter elegance." My recollection of the home at Palm Springs is dim, as I was only there for an hour or so, but Graceland is deeply imbedded in my mind because it was my second home for months, and I still visit there at least a couple of times a month. As we left the home in Palm Springs, I told Katey to pick up one of the green stones on the lawn and save it for a souvenir. We piled back in the wagon and headed for the airport, passing Colonel Tom Parker's house, which was dark at that hour; it appeared to be white stucco and a good size.

We boarded the plane at 2 a.m. Memphis time, and headed home. There were no pillows on the plane, but Elvis had the fellows take off their jackets, which he rolled up and brought to me to use as a pillow. He insisted that Katey and I stretch out on the long couch and take a nap because we both had to work that day. We dozed on the trip home. I was still dozing when Elvis shook my shoulder at 5:15 a.m. to say we were home.

Billy Smith, Elvis' cousin, was at the airport when we arrived home, and we piled in the limo and headed for Graceland. Katey and I were both wide awake and still thrilled over the "fairy tale" trip we had been on.

When we arrived at the mansion, I stopped by the kitchen, before going upstairs to bathe, to ask Pauline if she would make a pot of coffee and fix Katey and me some breakfast. Katey went on up with me and stretched out across Lisa's bed while I bathed. Before we went back downstairs, I stopped in Elvis' room to give him some medicine. He was already in bed, and Katey wanted to thank him for the trip and the bracelet. To the best of my recollection, Katey never saw Elvis again, but like me, his memory lives in her heart.

We went downstairs and had breakfast, then Katey dropped me off at the hospital before she went on home to get ready for work. I was on duty at the time, and not only the girls but also the doctors who came up on the floor that day were excited to hear about our trip. I had called Bob and my mother, so they both knew that we were home safely. Katey got home about the time I was talking to Bob. What a grand and memorable trip this was!

Elvis in concert in Memphis, 1976—*Photo by Jerry R. Larson.*

Elvis in concert in Memphis, 1976—*Photo by Jerry R. Larson.*

Elvis in concert in Memphis, 1976—*Photo by Jerry R. Larson.*

Marian leaving the Baptist Memorial Hospital—*Photo by Gil Michael.*

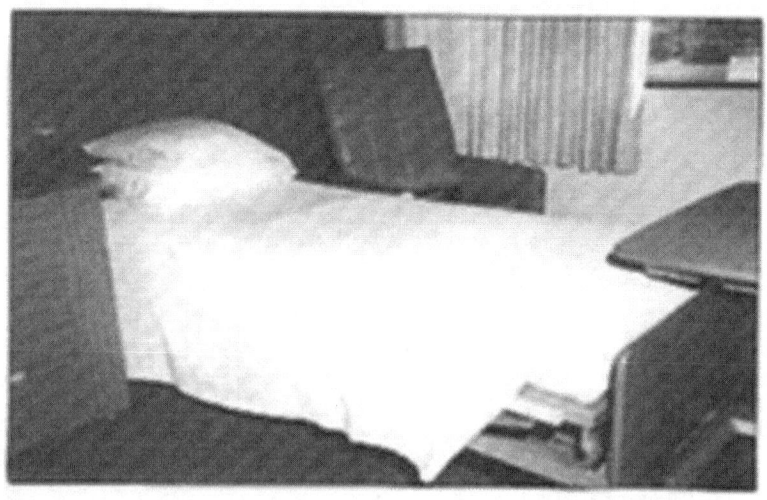

The bedroom of the suite Elvis used at Baptist Memorial Hospital—*Photo by Stuart Hooser.*

The sitting room of the suite Elvis used at Baptist Memorial Hospital—*Photo by Stuart Hooser.*

Marian's mother, Nocal Justice—*From the author's collection.*

Marian at her office, Baptist Memorial Hospital—*Photo by Gil Michael.*

Marian at home—*Photo by Gil Michael.*

Marian and her husband, Bob with one of their dogs—*Photo by Gil Michael.*

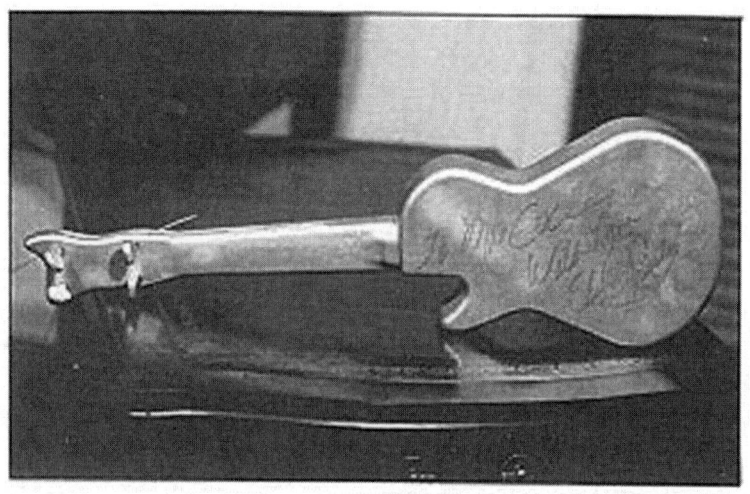

This small guitar came on a basket of flowers, and Elvis inscribed it to Marian—*Photo by Gil Michael.*

Photo montage inscribed to Marian by Elvis—
Photo by Gil Michael.

Marian's 1976 Pontiac Grand Prix that Elvis gave her—*Photo by Gil Michael.*

The fabulous mink presented to Marian by Elvis—*Photo by Gil Michael.*

Elvis in concert in Memphis, 1976—*Photo by Jerry R. Larson.*

6. My Mother's Illness

*I*n October of 1975, I went to Dallas to visit my sister, Catherine Vonder Hoya, and her family. Elvis told me to call him while I was gone in order to let him know how I was doing. I went to Dallas on October 15, and on the 16th, my sister Patty called from Memphis to say that Mother was in the hospital for what they thought was a pulmonary embolus of the right lung. Mother had not wanted Patty to let me know this because she thought I should be allowed to enjoy my vacation, but Patty knew I would be furious if she didn't let me know, so she called.

I immediately placed a call to our good friend and physician, Dr. Gerald Plitman. He asked how I knew that Mother was in the hospital; she had told him that day when she went to the office that she had felt bad for several days, but was waiting until I left town to come to him. This way she felt she would assure my having a vacation. He told me that he had sent her down for a lung scan, for her chest X-ray had shown a mass in her lower right lung. The pulmonary scan also showed this mass, and he thought it might be an embolus. Dr. Plitman said he had started her on heparin, a medication that is a blood thinner and administered intravenously (we call that IV), and that he was observing her closely. I then called my mother and asked her where she got off being so smart and not letting me know she felt bad. She was pleased I called, although she wouldn't admit it. She spoke to Catherine too, and then assured both of us that she was fine and enjoying her rest. She insisted that I not return to Memphis because of her illness.

I could tell by the telephone number of her room that she had a private room on my floor, but I knew it was an inside room and I wanted something better for her so she would have a pleasant view rather than just looking out on the "back yard" of the hospital. As I had planned to call Elvis anyway, I did not call the floor at the hospital. Rather I called Elvis and asked that he and Kathy take care of getting her changed to a better room the following morning, which he did. I talked to him for ten or fifteen minutes while my sister Catherine and her son John listened in on the extension so they could hear his voice. John could hardly wait to tell his friends that he had heard the sound of Elvis' voice over the phone. Later that night some friends of Catherine's and Fred's came over, and when John told them one man asked me how I had managed to call and get through to Elvis. I explained that I had just picked up the phone and dialed the number, but he could hardly believe that I had no problem getting to speak to Elvis.

During our phone conversation, Elvis told me to stay in Dallas and enjoy my visit, saying he would take care of things, that it was not necessary for me to come home. He said if it did become necessary for me to go home, he would send the *Jet Star* for me. And he said he really missed me and would be glad when I got back to town.

I flew home earlier than I had planned to, but didn't let Mother know it. As far as she knew, I would be in on Sunday morning and come in after church to see her; Daddy and Patty, Katcy, and Bob kept quiet about me coming home early.

On Sunday when we went to the hospital, she really looked quite well and relaxed. We (Catherine and I) had gotten gifts in Dallas for her and Daddy, so I took those to the hospital. We stayed for a nice visit, then went on home. Mother asked me if I was going to resume my nightly trips to Graceland, and I asked if she wouldn't like for me to stay with her. She said no, that she wanted me to see about Elvis because he really needed me.

I went back to Graceland around 7:00 p.m. and was given a royal welcome. Everyone was as glad to see me as I was to see them, and I brought small gifts for Elvis, Delta, Lisa, Kathy, and Grandma. We sat up all night and talked. I was still on vacation, so I didn't have to meet any deadlines.

On Monday morning around 9:00 when I got up (I had gotten to bed around 5 a.m.), I bathed and dressed, checked on Elvis, called home, went downstairs to breakfast, and left for the hospital. Mother was feeling good and was up and about. Dr. Plitman had been in and had ordered more lab studies on her, but she was really feeling so well that she wanted to go home. I stayed with her until one or two o'clock, then went on home and told her I would be back early the next morning so I could see the doctor. When I got home, Bob and I went out for a drive, then came home and I cooked dinner. When Katey got home from work, we all sat around and had a nice visit. I told them more about my trip to Dallas. I had given them their gifts when I got back, and then I again headed for Graceland.

Elvis was asleep when I arrived at the house, so after depositing my fresh clothes for the next day in Lisa's room, I went downstairs, going by the kitchen for a cup of coffee and then in to visit with Delta and Grandma. I stayed with them until Elvis called down to let us know he was awake. I went up to Lisa's room, called for our usual pot of coffee, and waited for the boy. When he came in, he was wearing a blue velour robe over white nylon pajamas, barefooted and with that shock of black hair falling over his left eye. He wanted to know about my mother and any pending studies to be done and asked me to keep him informed. I told him I was going in early the next day so I could see the doctor.

We spent a quiet evening, just visiting, drinking our coffee, and then watching football on TV. He was going out after the ball game to play racquet ball, then take in a movie, and I went on to bed. Elvis never left the house at night without first coming back to my room to say goodnight.

Tuesday morning when I got to the hospital, around 8:30 a.m., I met Dr. Plitman in the hall. He had already been in to see Mother and he said that she had decreased breath sounds on the right lung and was sending her down for a chest X-ray. She went down for this, and after she returned to her room, we just enjoyed each other's company the rest of the morning. I went down to the drugstore and got a sandwich and took it back to her room so I could eat with her; then after lunch she wanted to take a nap before some of her bridge cronies came up to visit so I went on home.

Shortly after I got home, probably around 2 p.m., Dr. Plitman called the house to say that there appeared to be something in Mother's right lung other than an embolus and he wanted to call in a thoracic man. I asked that he call Dr. Jacob Rosensweig. I contemplated going back to the hospital, but knew that this would alarm Mother, and as Patty went by every afternoon, I knew that keeping things close to normal was the way to go. Just a few minutes after I talked to Dr. Plitman, the phone rang; it was Elvis. Could I come on out? I went out to Graceland after calling Dr. Rosensweig to let him know where I would be, and then I called Mother to let her know that the new doctor would be by to see her; I told her that the area in her lung where the embolus had been located was still present and that Dr. Plitman wanted Dr. Rosensweig to see and to look at the X-rays. She took the news calmly enough, and I told her I would call her back later.

Approximately an hour later. Dr. Rosensweig called me at Graceland to say that he had sent Mother down for tomagrams (special detail X-rays), and that what had appeared to be embolus was instead a mass which seemed to be the size of an orange. I asked him if she was apprehensive, and he said not at all, that he had told her he would have to do a bronchoscopy on her the next day, and that he would have to have her given a general anesthetic. She took this calmly too. I called her, and she was quite chipper. I offered to go in and stay with her, but she said no, that she was fine. Elvis and I sat and talked for a long time, and he really worked overtime to keep me occupied. We talked about everything from soup to nuts. Then around 7 p.m. he called the kitchen for his usual meal and told Lottie to fix me a big thick T-bone. Our evening went as most others went. Vernon came over to visit for awhile, and I excused myself and went down to visit Grandma and Delta. I had come to really care about these two ladies, and I thoroughly enjoyed my visits with them. Then I called my mother; daddy and Patty were there, and she was fine.

Wednesday morning I went to the hospital very early to be there before Mother went to surgery. Patty, my sister, came shortly after I got there. We had asked Daddy not to come as we knew the wait would be hard on him, and he would do better to stay busy. She went down to the operating room around 10 a.m., and it wasn't long before Dr. Rosensweig came up to say that she was in the recovery room. He had bad news for us, which I had anticipated. He said the bronchoscopy, which he had just completed, would have to be followed by a thorocotomy (which means to open the chest). The night before, I had called my brothers and other sister, alerting them to begin making their arrangements to come for I had anticipated the need for more surgery. I stayed at the hospital most of the day as Mother was groggy. Patty stayed too. Toward early evening we both left after Mother was awake and fine and wondering why we were still there. I went home first, then on to Graceland.

Shortly after I arrived at Graceland, I was sitting in Lisa's room when Elvis came in. He walked over to my chair, which was where he usually sat, and knelt down on his knees, put his arm around my shoulders, and told me that he knew about my mother. He wanted me to know that he was available to go to the hospital at anytime, and he said that if there was anything that she or I needed, I was to come to him. I told him that his kind words and feeling meant more than anything else, that we, as a family, took care of our own, but it was nice to know we had a crutch if we needed it. That night he sat there with me all night and kept my mind occupied with stories about Hollywood and his various tours. The next day he sent Mother a huge bouquet of flowers. I called my brothers and sister once again and said that they should come right on home as Mother would be having her surgery on Monday (this was Thursday). They all came in the next day: Dick from Mississippi, Joe from Virginia, and Catherine from Dallas.

On that Friday morning I went to bed about 5 a.m. and got up around 8:00, bathed, and went downstairs for breakfast. I went back upstairs to Lisa's room, called my sister to meet me at the hospital, then checked in Elvis' room and he was sleeping, so I left.

Patty arrived at the hospital about the time I did, and I took her down to the suite, which was next to Mother's room. I showed her the large room, large sitting room, and two bathrooms; I told her I wanted to move Mother in there before the rest of the family got there because I knew we would need all the extra space we could get. We had talked to Mother about this the day before, but she had not wanted to move, saying it was "too expensive." I had checked with administration to see if we could use the sitting room only during the day of surgery, if the suite was not occupied, as we were such a large family, and I would pay for the use of that room for the day. They gave approval for the use of the room, but no charge was to be made. However, the next morning after talking to Patty, we decided to move Mother into the suite, but we had to convince her first that it was the logical thing to do. After she had breakfast and was awaiting Dr. Plitman, Dr. Rosensweig, and Dr. Leigh Adkins, I saw these men arrive at the nurses' station; then they stopped by to see her. They explained the surgery to her, which she took very well, but she asked if it was cancer. Dr. Rosenweig told her we would need the pathology reports after surgery to tell her all the information she would want; this also satisfied her. After they left, Patty and I took her in and showed her the suite, then gave her the old snow job about how much more comfortable we would all be, and she was sold. After all, the comfort of her family was what she had spent her life providing! She asked about the expense, so I told her that she had plenty of insurance. Patty and I had already decided that she, Dick, and I would take care of the difference. When we told my daddy that he said, "No way. I will pay Mama's bills!" All the clan came home. Catherine did not bring her family at that time, but Dick did bring his, although

Doris took the girls home (back to Waynesboro for Jill and Susan back to Ole Miss).

Jenny Wood, one of Mother's closest friends, and wife of our retired minister, was admitted to the hospital and was on my floor. She asked to be taken to Mother's room, and when Dr. Wood took her, in a wheel chair, to Mother's suite, Jenny said, "Nocal, I really came to see you, but I have to go to the bathroom." When she came out, she grinned at Mother and said, "I really just wanted to use the same pot that Elvis had used." Dr. Wood got a kick out of telling that story, and when I told Elvis, he really enjoyed it.

I was still going to Graceland during all of this, but told Mother that when she had her surgery I would be staying with her. She said I could stay for a few nights, but I needed to get back to Graceland. I talked to Elvis that night and told him that I would be gone for awhile. He asked me if I would drive out for an hour or so each night just to take a break from being in the hospital twenty-four hours a day, which I did. I stayed at Graceland through Saturday night and spent Sunday night at the hospital. I did go out to Graceland on Sunday night for an hour or so, taking Catherine with me. I told Elvis not to get sick as he wouldn't have a suite to go to because we had moved Mother in. He said, "If I get sick, you'll have to move in a bed for me because I go where you are." Once again, he sent her flowers.

On Monday morning at 10:00, Mother was taken to surgery. Dr. Roy Stauffer, our minister, and another Dr. Roy Stauffer, a physician and cousin to our minister, along with Dr. Plitman went to the operating room with Mother. They each kissed her before they took her into the OR; when she came back and had rested for several hours, she quipped that she had been the envy of all those pretty young nurses in the OR.

Louise Courtney, the OR supervisor, and Joyce Ann Robinson, her assistant, had told me that during the operation they would call me every thirty minutes to let me know how things were going. The initial call came to say that the chest had been opened and they were going in. The second call came as scheduled to say that she was doing okay. The third call did not come, and when the thirty minutes had passed, I knew that Mother had been an "open and close"—the tumor was too large for removal, and the disease had spread too far. I walked out to the nurses' station and asked Pat Brownlow, the RN in charge that day, if she had heard anything. She said no.

A few minutes later, the door to the sitting room opened, and Dr. Rosensweig came in. Everyone then knew what I had already expected. He had cautioned the recovery room not to call the floor (as is the policy) to let us know that Mother was in there. He felt that he should be there to talk to us first, and he knew that we would know it was all bad if recovery called.

The days that followed were good, despite the terrible cloud we were under. Mother really recuperated from the actual surgery with amazing speed. All of us were still there, and she thrived when all her family got together. I had asked my LPN's if they would do private duty with Mother for a couple of days, using their days off and letting us pay them, which they did. I chose these ladies because they had taken care of her before surgery, and I knew they would have a special interest in her as a person as well as a patient—not that my RN's wouldn't, but the LPN's really have more patient contact. I stayed day and night too, leaving only an hour or so each night to go to Graceland. Bob and Katey, in the meantime, had not been cast off. I was still being with them, as they were at the hospital daily, and never one time was there a complaint from either of them.

The hospital was great! Dr. Frank Groner, the administrator, was extremely thoughtful, which we appreciated. The hospital hostess brought Mother a large stuffed toy from the play room, which she named "Gip," initials G.I.P., for Gerald I. Plitman — and everyone on the floor who came in, and she thought about it, wrote on her toy. The various administrators and chief nurses came by, as did many other people from throughout the hospital who knew me. Roy Stauffer, our minister, was there often, as were others from the church. Dr. Roy Stauffer, the physician, came a couple of times daily. Mother told him that if he would stay in Memphis when he completed his residency, she would adopt him! I now call him my "adopted baby brother!" He is a close family friend and spent Christmas with us last year. The girls on the floor really showered her with attention, and things went right along. After four days she told me it was time for me to go back to Graceland at night, and Patty wanted to stay with Mother. I conceded and went back to my other "patient."

Mother was in the hospital a month, or thereabouts, starting on X-ray therapy as an "inpatient," and, after discharge, finishing it as an "outpatient." Elvis called her during this period of time and again sent flowers. The first night he called her, she spent fifteen minutes telling him how he needed to slow up and get his rest.

Life fell back into its regular pattern. I was back on duty, stopped every afternoon on the way home from the hospital to visit with Mother and Daddy for an hour or so, going on home to fix dinner and be with my family, then on to Graceland. Mother was not very strong and unable to do anything. Patty did most of the cooking for her, with Daddy and me helping out. He had bought her a ceramic-top stove with a self-cleaning oven for her birthday on December 3rd, and she was able to use it only one time; somehow or other she got into the kitchen one afternoon while Daddy was downstairs doing laundry and fixed him country fried steak because she knew how badly he wanted that. When I got to the apartment, I finished it up for her. She could go to the kitchen and get a glass of milk and a bowl of cereal, or cheese and crackers, but she was not very strong and required much help.

Elvis sent her roses. He was such a considerate boy. He called her one night; she was pleased that he would do such a thing. The night before her birthday, he (without knowing her birth date) sent her a Christmas tape and autographed it. By his thoughtfulness he really helped my family through this difficult period — and those yet to come.

7.   The Christmas Of 1975

*J*ust after Thanksgiving, Elvis was due to go to Las Vegas for a two-week stint. He called and asked me to come out that night to visit with him until it was time for him to leave. I got out to Graceland around 9:00 p.m., and we sat with our usual pot of coffee and visited until nearly midnight. This was his first performance since his illness, and he appeared a little uptight. In fact, when I got to the door, I could almost feel the tension in the house. I stopped by the kitchen first to ask if the "boss" was awake and to ask Maggie to bring us a pot of coffee.

Everyone in the kitchen was unusually quiet, and I asked what was up. No one knew, they said. I went on upstairs and was putting my coat up when Maggie came in with the coffee. She would usually stop and talk for a few minutes, but she scurried out immediately. As I walked over to the couch, Elvis walked in — no, he stormed in. Never in my life had I seen anyone any angrier. I had seen him "hacked off" before, although never with me, but this particular night he was angry and really "uptight." He sat down, and I very quietly "lathered" (creamed and sugared) his coffee. I didn't open my mouth. He sat there for a minute or two, literally seething, and then he mumbled, "She doesn't own me." He made a couple of more comments, and I still never opened my mouth.

Just about the time he seemed to be ready to talk and was settled down enough to drink his coffee, Dr. Nick walked in, and Elvis immediately clammed up. Dr. Nick sat down on Lisa's bed and looked at me questioningly and asked if he had interrupted anything. Elvis got up and walked out. I told Dr. Nick that all I could say was Elvis was upset and had just begun to open up when he walked in, so I didn't know what was wrong. Dr. Nick then left. I didn't know what to do and soon I got uptight. A short time later, Elvis came in to say he was going to get a haircut, that he would be right back, and would I call for another pot of coffee. All I had been able to determine at this point about the problem was that it involved Linda.

I went downstairs for a few minutes, and when I started back upstairs, Linda walked in the front door. Did she look awful! She had been crying; her eyes were really swollen from her copious tears, and her face was all blotched! I stopped and asked her what in the world was wrong, and she said that she couldn't tell me. I asked, "Why, what the heck is going on?" She replied that she had promised she wouldn't tell me. I asked if it involved me, if that was the reason I wasn't supposed to know about it. With that she burst into tears and told me what was wrong, asking me please not to let Elvis know that she had told me. I told her that I felt he had been about to tell me when Dr. Nick came in. I do not intend to divulge all of the details here because, although it has been a long time now, it could still affect lives.

While Linda was telling me this, Elvis walked in and the subject was dropped like a hot potato with not another word said. He was glad to see Linda, and the three of us sat there and visited like nothing had happened. They were leaving at midnight and Elvis gave me a big bear hug, a kiss on the cheek, and walked me downstairs to the car, telling me I should call him if I needed anything or got lonesome.

The two weeks my Babe was gone, I called Graceland daily to check on Grandma and Delta and got lots of rest. I didn't call Elvis while he was gone as I felt he needed all the rest he could get, but I sent him a wire saying, "The city is dark and quiet — my shining star is away and I miss you."

About 9:30 on the morning of December 14, I was at work when the phone rang and that soft voice said, "Mrs. Cocke, I'm home. Will you get here as early as you can tonight?" This reminds me of one day when the phone rang at the nurses' station and my transcriber, JoAnn Berlenski, answered it, after which she came to my office to say that "some man" wanted to speak to me. She apologized for disturbing me while I was eating my lunch and said she had started not to bother me with the phone call but was afraid it might be important. I answered the phone to hear that soft voice asking if I was busy. "I'm eating my lunch," I replied. After listening some more, I said, "Sure, honey, I'll be down in a few minutes."

When I hung up the phone, JoAnn, in her high, excited voice, asked, "Who was that?" When I told her it was Elvis, she grabbed her head with both hands and said, "Oh, no! And I didn't even know I was talking to him!" JoAnn died the first part of the year 1977. She was only thirty-one years old.

Back to the night of December 14, I once again headed for what had been my second home for several months. I stopped by Grandma's room to see her and Delta for a few minutes, then headed upstairs. As I was taking off my coat, Elvis came in, gave me a big bear hug and a kiss on the cheek, and we settled down for a cup of coffee and a long visit. He told me about his two weeks in Las Vegas and asked about my mother and how I had been. He then told me what had made him so uptight that day he had left for Las Vegas, and the incident was never mentioned again.

Soon we were settled into the same routine we had followed earlier: me going out to Graceland and us frequently talking much of the night. When I had to get up early to go to work, I'd run downstairs as soon as I got up, start the percolator, put two strips of bacon in a skillet, set the burner on low, then go back upstairs to bathe and dress. One morning I came down and there was Charlie Hodge fixing my breakfast. He did this for me on several occasions and was very thoughtful. However, Pauline, the night lady, would always have my breakfast ready if I would let her know the night before that I had to get up and go to work.

I have many memories of this period. For example, one afternoon about 4:00 o'clock, when I got home from work, Bob said that Elvis had just called and wanted to know if I could come out a little earlier than usual. I called Graceland to see if everything was okay. Elvis was fine, saying he had something he wanted me to see and could I come out pretty soon. I started dinner for Bob and Katey; then Bob said he would finish it, and I left for Graceland. There I went upstairs, and he was waiting for me in Lisa's room. He said, "Come on, let's go," grabbed my hand, and tore off down the stairs. In the back yard were three three-wheeled cycles. Linda and David Leech were on one, with Linda the operator, Billy Smith and his wife Jo were on the other, and Elvis and I got on the third. He looked back to me, "Hang on, Mrs. Cocke," and away we went!

We drove out the back gate, turned right onto the highway, then right again on Old Hickory, and he opened the thing up. Whee! What a ride. I was really hanging on. We were approaching an intersection where we had to turn right or left, and there was a stop sign. Elvis slowed down some, looked back at me, and asked "Are you okay?" I answered yes — when suddenly brakes screamed. I hung on tighter to keep from flying over his head. He looked back at me, grinned that famous grin, and commented, "Oh my gosh! We almost got creamed."

A lady had almost hit us. She was far more shook up than we were. Elvis grinned at her, waved, and we took off again. A friend told me later that she had seen me "flying down the highway" on a three-wheeler with Elvis Presley and couldn't believe her eyes.

The next ten days there was hustle and bustle at Graceland getting ready for Christmas. I had gotten Elvis white nylon pajamas and a blue velour robe; I also had gifts for Grandma, Delta, Lisa, Linda, and all the five maids. On Christmas Eve I got to the house very late, for I had gone with Bob and Katey to see Mother and Daddy; my brothers, sisters, and their families were all home as usual for Christmas, and Bob and Katey started home when I left for Graceland. I told all of them I would see them at Mother's and Daddy's at 7:00 a.m. on Christmas Day.

Graceland was packed with people when I arrived. There was all sorts of food out on the counters in the kitchen, and there must have been at least a hundred people there. I went on up to Lisa's room and in just a few minutes Elvis came in — furious! I sat very quietly and waited for him to speak. I poured our coffee, "lathered" his, and put it over within his reach and waited for him to speak.

He told me he had had a dream which had been so real to him that he had awakened in a rage. He had dreamed that no one who worked for him cared anything about him other than for their salary checks. He had dreamed that he had gone broke, and when he needed them they walked out on him. In his dream during this turmoil, he said that I had walked in and said, "Babe, everything's okay." With that, he laughed and we just sat there and visited.

This particular night, he asked me what I thought of the boys — how I felt about each of them. I gave him my honest opinion. He called the roll. Dick; I said fine. Al; I said good boy. Billy Smith; very fine and devoted to Elvis. So it went down the roll until we got to Dave, Red, and Sonny; these three bothered me mainly because I actually liked Red and Sonny, but I told Elvis that I felt that their loyalty went only as far as the paychecks. (We discussed that statement in August of 1977 when their book appeared in print. Elvis asked if I thought the book would hurt him and how I felt about it. I told him that no one or nothing in any way could ever change the way I felt about him and that I believed this would be the way his fans would react. My main thought about the book was this: how could anything or anyone destroy your love and respect for someone just because someone else had no loyalty. I told Elvis that the three writers would only hurt themselves.)

I called the kitchen for more coffee and for his breakfast, and I expect we sat there until two or three o'clock. By then most of the folks downstairs had gone home, but those closest to him had stayed, and he had gifts for them. Afterward he went to his room. Vernon and Sandy were in there, as was Linda, and I went on to bed. I must have slept or dozed at least a couple of hours when Lisa came in and woke me up to say that Santa Claus had come, so I put on my robe and went downstairs.

Lisa was bouncing around looking at her gifts, and Elvis, Linda, and David Leech were there. There was a package under the tree for me, a white knit cape. Elvis opened my gift to him and immediately went in and changed his pajamas and robe to the ones I had given him. He came back in and said to me, "Mrs. Cocke, Christmas isn't over yet," to which I replied, "You're right, honey. It will be here all day." I didn't know then what he meant. I left Graceland around 6:30 a.m. and went on over to my folks. That was my mother's last Christmas, and, when we all went in, she was sitting on the couch drinking a cup of hot tea. She had on a pink robe I had given her, and there were tears in her eyes. It was a hard day for all of us, yet we made the most of it and stored many precious memories to go with those we had stored up during our lifetimes.

Christmas night I once again headed for Graceland. I was really tired and hoped that all was quiet so that I could get to bed early. I felt that Elvis would probably have his special friends in. Although he had always made me a part of any group if I so chose, I knew I wanted to hit the sack early. I went right upstairs after stopping in to see Grandma and Delta. Linda came in right after I got there, and she stretched across Lisa's bed and I on the day bed. We were both tired, but Elvis came in and told us both to get up because we were going out. We asked him if we had to, and he said yes.

I went in the bathroom to freshen up, and when I came out he was standing there holding my coat. We went on downstairs. There was Dr. Nick and Edna (his wife), Paul and Pearl Schoeffer, T. J. Shepard and his wife, plus all of the boys, Vernon, Sandy, and Lori, Sandy's little girl, and Lisa. Elvis announced that we were going to the airport, so we went out to go in the limo and his Stutz was there. He was driving, and said I should go with him. When we got out to the *Lisa Marie*, the pilots were there and the plane was ready for take off. I didn't know where we were going and really didn't care; I just knew I wanted to take a nap, so I promptly curled up on a couch and went to sleep. I think we went to Nashville, and Lamar Fike, who worked for him, but lived in Nashville, was there to meet the plane. I think this is what went on; while everyone else was having a good time, I was sacked out asleep.

Sometime around 4:30, someone awakened me to say we were back in Memphis. I sat up and was putting my shoes on when Linda came in and told me that Elvis wanted me. I went back to his room, and he was standing there with a big smile on his face. He said, "Mrs. Cocke, come here." Lowell Hayes was standing in the doorway to the dressing room and Linda was there. Elvis told me to close my eyes and put out my hand which he promptly took and slipped a ring on my finger; then he told me I could open my eyes. My knees buckled when I saw the ring! I was dazzled by the beauty of it! He caught me, hugged me close, and said, "Mrs. Cocke, you are very special to me, but don't show your present to anyone else until they get theirs because they might not like theirs if they see yours first." My ring was a twenty-one carat aquamarine, circled with two carats of diamonds. The aquamarine is emerald-cut in four tiers, and the diamonds are baguettes and point stones. The next to get rings were T. J. Shepard and his wife. Theirs were matching rings, gold with seven small diamonds; oh, how they raved over those rings.

I kept my hand in my pocket.

The next couple was Paul and Pearl Schoeffer. His ring was much like T. J.'s. Pearl's was a black onyx, a

115

very thin stone circled with diamonds. Pearl carried on so about her ring! She hugged Elvis about four times and she said to him, "I could hug you all night." He looked at me and said, "She probably would too if I'd stand still."

They both laughed. I kept my hand in my pocket.

Then came Dr. Nick and Edna. Her ring was much like the one he had given T. J.'s wife; he gave Dr. Nick a watch with small diamonds circling the face. They were pleased, and I kept my hand in my pocket.

The last one was Delta, and she was as surprised over the whole thing as I was. She, like me, never knew we were getting such fabulous gifts. Her ring was a square, no, oblong-shaped opal circled with diamonds. I still had my hand in my pocket! We all went into the conference room of the plane, each showing the other his gift until someone turned to me and said, "What did you get? Let's see it."

I took my hand out of my pocket, extended it for all to see, and you could have heard a pin drop. There was total silence until someone found words to say, "Good night! What a rock!" Elvis was right, but everyone thought the gifts were great and everyone had received beautiful gifts. T. J. Shepard had never been very cordial because I didn't know him well, had been around him very little, and once — unknowingly — had insulted him.

What had happened with T. J. was this. One day during Elvis' hospitalization in August, a young man and woman had come to the nursing station and asked if

Elvis was awake. I said no. The man asked if Dean was there and would I call him to the desk, which I did. When Dean got to the desk, he greeted the couple warmly and then turned to me and said rather abruptly, "Why didn't you tell me who was out here?" To this I replied, "Because I don't know who they are." Dean and the other man just looked at me. Dean said, "This is T. J. Shepard and his wife," to which I replied, "Oh well, how do you do." I had never heard of T. J. and wasn't impressed with the name. Later when I told Elvis about the incident, he laughed. He said that he had known T. J. a long time although they were not bosom buddies.

There was much chattering about our gifts, but no one could believe I had been given such a fabulous ring.

It was around 5:30 a.m. by then. I had to go to work, so I asked David Leech to drive me to Graceland so I could get ready for work. It only took a few minutes to get to the house where I bathed, dressed, and went on to work. Did I cause a rage of excitement! Everyone came to my floor just to see my ring, and the magnificence of it went through the hospital like wildfire. I had called my mother and told her about it, also Bob and Katey, so all were anxious to see it as soon as I got off.

When I got in to report that afternoon about 2:40 p.m., Kathy Seamon was sitting there. She had already heard about my ring. I showed it to her, and she said that she thought it was beautiful and that I deserved it. Kathy's husband was being transferred, so she had stopped going to Graceland quite a while before Christmas. The following Monday morning one of the oncologists came to the floor and asked to see my gift. He said that Dr. Nick had told everyone at the office that Elvis had given me the most beautiful ring he had ever seen.

The next few days at Graceland were much the same as always. Elvis was going to Detroit, Michigan, for a single New Year's Eve performance. He was flying up that evening and would be back the next night so I didn't go out to the house. I had to work and couldn't make the trip although he had invited me to go. When he came back to town the morning of January 2, he again called to say he was home and I went out that night. As I was off duty the next day, we sat up all night and visited. He and Linda told me about the concert while we drank coffee.

8. My Mother's Death

a couple of days after the excitement of Christmas subsided, I left Graceland, not to return on a nightly basis again. I wanted to be with my mother as much as possible, so I packed my bags and moved into the suite on my floor, along with my sister Pat. Bob and Katey came often, took care of our laundry, and ran errands. Daddy came every night. Catherine flew in from Dallas at least a couple of times that month, and Joe came from Virginia and Dick from Mississippi. Mother was receiving X-ray treatment for her hip because the disease was spreading, and she was given an injection of three chemo drugs. Days and nights were mighty bleak, but Patty and I were always in attendance.

I took a leave of absence from work, although I was on the floor and available for consultation all the time. Patty also took a leave. We encouraged Daddy to work during the day because he did better not to have to stay in so close, but he called several times a day, we called him often, and he was there every night. My daddy is a retired Army Colonel who didn't like being idle, so he worked as a volunteer at Veterans' Administration hospital and also worked for a men's clothing store part-time.

We stayed at the hospital from January 1, 1976, until January 31st, when we took Mother home. I had not been to my own house for nearly five weeks, but saw Bob and Katey almost daily. Katey still worked at Helen of Memphis, which was just a half block from where Mother and Daddy lived, so she could come over for lunch. In the meantime, Elvis had called several times and I had called him, and he had also sent flowers a couple of times. I was still on leave of absence, as was Patty, and Daddy told them at the store and at the hospital that he wouldn't be back as long as he was needed at home. Thus the three of us were always on hand. Patty did most of the kitchen work and the cooking, and she would go by her office every day for a short time; she is the director of a school for retarded children, Forget Me Not, Inc. Daddy did the dishes, cleaning, laundry, and anything else he could find to keep busy. Me? I had the privilege of taking care of Mother — and this was truly a privilege.

Mother asked me if she was going to die. The morning she asked me this, we were alone. There was no way I would insult her intelligence by telling her "no," so I told her the truth. She asked me if it would be easier on me if she went back to the hospital so I could work if I wanted to. I asked where she preferred to be, and she said, "Home!" She had two things to ask of me: one, not to let anyone try to prolong her life once she passed thru that doorway, and two, not to let her suffer. She had my word.

On the 9th of February, we called Dick to come home. It was Patty's birthday. We knew that the end was approaching for Mother, and we knew that she would like to have some time to spend with Dick. We called him that morning early, and he was there before supper that night. He didn't leave until February 25th. On Thursday, the 12th of February, we called Catherine to come home. Then on Sunday, the 15th, we called Joe, and he came home that night from Virginia. By this time, Mother was completely bedridden and required more medication for pain. She slept and dreamed a lot, and we watched her slip from us daily.

Thursday night, the 19th, was very bad for her. Dr. Plitman came by, as he had done many times without us calling for him, and he told us what we already knew: that the end — no the beginning — for her was closely approaching. On Friday morning she called all of us to her bedside to say that she loved us and to tell us how much fun it had been to be with all of us. She wanted to see Emilie Bowerman, her closest friend, and she wanted to thank Catherine Phillips for all her attentions to her "before I cross over the bridge." I had the operator interrupt Mrs. Bowerman, who was on the phone, so I could call her over, and Dick went down the hall to get Catherine. Mother, Daddy, and Patty live in a high rise, with Patty's apartment next door to theirs. Dick and our Catherine were staying in Patty's place.

After Mother spoke to her two friends, as she had spoken to Daddy and her five "kids," she never said another word, but slipped into a semi-comatose state. On Monday morning at 1:54 a.m., February 23rd, with Daddy and her five children present, Our Lord took Mother from us. She went as quietly and as gently as a candle that burns out. We all cried because this precious life had been taken from us, but we said "The Lord's Prayer," each of us kissed Mother and told her goodnight, not good-bye, then we sat in the living room waiting for our minister, Roy Stauffer, and Dr. Nick. He was on call for the medical group, and he came to legally pronounce Mother dead. To this day, my daddy never says "Mama died." He says, "Since Mama went away."

That day and the next were busy. There were many friends coming in with food, flowers, and condolences. Mother was laid to rest on the 24th, and once again we adjusted to our situation. Elvis didn't come, but he, as well as Delta and Grandma, sent flowers. Elvis sent a six-foot-tall stand that must have had three hundred carnations, white mums, and a white dove. Things took a new pace for me. I was at home again, and there was no need for me to continue going to Graceland. Elvis was doing quite well. I had really been more a confidant and companion to him than a nurse the last few weeks of my stay at Graceland, and he was going on tour taking a number of trips. Thus I didn't see him for some time. Oh, I was still a frequent visitor to Graceland. I went often for lunch and to visit with Delta and Grandma and stayed one night when he was out of town and Grandma was ill. Dr. Nick was with Elvis, so when Delta called to say Grandma was ill, I called Vince Smith, a medical resident on Dr. Nick's service, and asked him to go to Graceland with me. Grandma really liked Vince, and now that he is in private practice, he has become her physician. He calls them "Miss Grandma" and "Miss Delta."

Marian's father, Howard Justice—*From the author's collection.*

9. Another Hospital Stay

uring the year 1976 I made many trips to Graceland and the year came and went quietly. In April of 1977 I received a call that Elvis was coming to the hospital. I had been made Administrative Supervisor of the sixteenth and seventeenth floors the first of 1977, so Elvis did not go to the 18ME but to 16ME. He had always told me that he went where I was, so when the man in the suite on the eighteenth floor offered to change with him, he declined and told him that his nurse had moved to the 16th floor.

He checked into the hospital around 6 a.m. and looked good. I was happy to see him and was given the customary hug and got him settled. We spent the whole morning talking, as I was to work in the Nursing Office that day on the 3-11 shift, so I was free that morning. He went to sleep around noon and that sleep lasted twenty-four hours. In the meantime the TV crews again came over, and I was interviewed. I slept at the hospital that night, as I had in the past, and worked 7-3 the next day. As 16ME was one of my areas, I was in and out all day, then went home at 3 p.m. to return that night to our old pattern.

I told him during this visit of the admiration held for him by Dr. and Mrs. Wood and by Maurice Elliott's mother. He had me take the Woods a vase of flowers with a note, and sent Mrs. Elliott a planter and a note. He also asked me to take flowers to the nursing office and to the administrative offices with a note of thanks.

One day during this four-day stay, I was off duty and

we were in the sitting room. He looked at me, grinned, and reached for my hand. He asked to see my ring. I took it off and handed it to him. He sorta grinned at me and asked where I got it. I said, "A rich old boyfriend gave it to me." He said, "Does this tell you how that rich old boy feels about you?" and I said, "Yes."

Then he said, "Where did you get that chain?" and I said, "The same old boy, but he put it on me, and I've never taken if off. Does that tell you how I feel about him?"

He smiled and said, "Yes, ma'am." That was my "TLC" chain. I still haven't taken it off.

Elvis stayed in the hospital four days and the morning he decided to go home, he came in my room, patted my hand to wake me and, very softly, he said, "Mrs. Cocke, I'm going home. I'll see you later." It was four a.m. I said okay and promptly went back to sleep.

The following day I was going to a middle management meeting at 10:00 a.m. when the operator paged me. It was Elvis. What time did I get off duty and would I please come out to Graceland that afternoon? I said yes, and asked if he was okay. He said that he was fine, but he wanted me to come out.

When I got out to Graceland, I went to see Grandma and Delta first. Delta said that Priscilla was upstairs with Elvis and that she would let him know I was there. She called him, and he asked that I wait a few minutes before coming up. I visited with them about fifteen minutes when he called down and asked that I come up.

I went directly to Lisa's room, knowing that this was where he would be, and when I walked in he gave me the usual bear hug and introduced me to Priscilla. She was lovely. He told her later that she was dressed and looked like someone out of "Doctor Zhivago," which had been my first impression. She greeted me warmly and said that she really already knew me because Elvis had spoken of me so frequently; she added that he was very fond of me, and she thanked me for always being on hand to take care of him. Billy Smith was also there.

I perched on the side of Lisa's bed, and we talked a few minutes. I told Priscilla that Elvis had always spoken only good things about her, in fact, only beautiful things to say where she was concerned. She said, "I thank you for that. What a lovely thing for you to say." We chatted a few minutes more, after which Elvis said to Priscilla, "Honey, have I ever told you how much this lady means to me and how good she has been to me?" to which Priscilla replied, "Many times." He said, "She has worked all day and taken care of me all night, and she has always come when I needed her." He then turned and told me, "Mrs. Cocke, that package on the bed is for you."

I had noticed the brown plastic bag on the bed when I walked in and only thought it was a hanging bag that Priscilla was taking back with her, for I knew that she was leaving that evening. The bag was a hanging coat bag from Goldsmiths. Billy was going to open it for me, but Elvis said, "No, let her do it." Inside was the most gorgeous silver-gray mink coat I have ever seen. The lining was almost as beautiful as the coat, silver-gray satin with appliqued roses, and in the right side of the coat was my name — Marian J. Cocke — beautifully monogrammed in a darker shade of gray. Inside the right pocket, the initials had been neatly stitched in. I was flabbergasted and could only gasp, then cry.

Elvis got up and helped me put it on; then he hugged me. I said, "Boy, I'm not gonna take it off!" He told me not to wear it to work the next day, because, if I did, every person at the hospital would come in with one like it the next day! We visited awhile longer, and he wanted to show me the new costume that had come in for the television show to be done during the June tour.

Elvis explained to Priscilla that during his hospital stay, he had told me that he had given Aunt Delta a mink coat and asked had I seen it. I had said yes, that it was beautiful, and that she was proud of it. He had said two or three other things about the coat, but I had made no comment. When he gave me mine, he said that he had tried to find out how much I liked Delta's for he wanted me to have one like it, but I hadn't given him much help.

While we were in the dressing room, Elvis asked me how many nurses had taken care of him besides me. I said, "Martin, Gina, Sue and Paula. He counted out a hundred dollars for each of them and asked that I take it to them the next day; then he tucked a hundred in the pocket of my coat and said that was for me. I told him there was no way that I wanted money, to which he replied, "The money is for taking care of me. The coat is for how I feel about you." We chatted for a few minutes longer, and he asked if I would come back in the next day or two. I said I would. I said my goodbyes to Priscilla and Billy and went on down to show Grandma and Delta my coat before I left. Vernon was there, and he also admired my coat.

When I got home, Katey was there, and she really flipped, as did Bob. I gave him the hundred dollars. In the days that followed, I went out to Graceland every two or three days to check on Elvis and to have a cup of coffee or a Pepsi with him. One day while I was at work, Elvis called to tell me that he had been in bed two days with a sprained ankle and would I please come out. When I got there, he was sitting up in the bed with his foot propped up on a pillow. His toes were discolored, and he was miserable.

I asked him who taped his foot, and he said one of the boys. I told him that the tape had to come off. I went into the bathroom, got a warm wash cloth and towel, a bottle of rubbing alcohol, and lotion. When I yanked off the tape, he exclaimed, "Whew! That smarts!" I washed his foot, switched to alcohol, and then put lotion on it. I noted that there was no swelling and that he probably had twisted his foot a little bit. The pain and discomfort were from the tight binding. After I gave his foot a good massage, he got up and said he was ready to go out and play racquet ball.

As June approached, Elvis was preparing to go on tour and was pleased that one of the networks would be filming one of the shows. The afternoon he was to leave he called me around 5:00 p.m. and wanted to know if I could come out before he left. I had just returned from the Veterans' Administration Hospital where my father had been operated on the previous day, and I was really worn out. I told Elvis that I was really bushed, to which he replied, "Well, I'll see you when I get back. What is your daddy's name?" I told him Daddy's name was Howard Justice, to which he responded, "Okay, take care of yourself, and I'll call you when I get home."

The next afternoon, when I got to Daddy's room, there was a large vase of flowers from Elvis. Daddy was pleased, and all of the nurses had come in to see the flowers and to ask Daddy why Elvis had sent him flowers. That was just one of the many thoughtful things that boy could think up to do for someone. Another example of his thoughtfulness was when he read in the paper about a young man who was in the VA hospital. He and his wife had been hurt, him critically, and things looked mighty bleak for them. Elvis sent them a check for a thousand dollars.

June and July were busy months for Bob and me. Our only child was getting married on July 9th to a young engineer from Knoxville, Tennessee, by the name of Rod. There were parties, luncheons, and teas to attend, and the time passed quickly. Elvis asked if I was pleased about the wedding, to which I replied, "Yes, Rod is a fine young man and we are very pleased about the wedding." Elvis asked if I would be offended if he did not come. I replied no, that it was Katey's and

Rod's day, and if he came, he would steal the show! He laughed at this.

During this period Ginger was at Graceland some of the times I went out, or she would come while I was there. I had met her while Elvis was in the hospital. I liked Ginger and she was always nice to me.

We talked of his forthcoming marriage (?) to her, and the main thing he said was, "I'm engaged, but. . . ."

Many times during the two and one-half years I was associated with him, he would ask if I would like to have specific things, to which I always said no. He would ask why, and I would tell him I had no use for them. I think the most treasured statement he ever made to me was the night he said, "Mrs. Cocke, you're one of the few people I know who has never asked anything of me but friendship." This is the "gift" that I have taken out of my treasure chest of memories and looked at many times. It is a gift that comforts me very much when I miss him the most — and, my, how I do miss being with him, hearing the sound of his voice, and seeing the twinkle in his eyes. As with my mother, the memory of him is etched in my mind and in my heart like filigreed gold. How nice it will be when I see them both again in that better world.

Other people were impressed when they learned about Elvis' gifts to me. For example, one day I was going down on the elevator at the hospital when John Quartermous, a new intern, got on. We spoke, and then he looked down at my hand and its ring and said, "Wow, that's the biggest diamond I've ever seen!" I told him what it was and who had given it to me. I was not as impressed with Elvis' gifts as I was by the feelings behind them.

My feeling was that the gifts he gave me were selected with feeling and then given with love. Had he given them to me because "I wanted them," they would have had no meaning. I expect that, if I had said "Great" to everything he had wanted to give me, I could have had almost anything I wanted. Let me say this about Elvis: he was an extremely generous person, but he never wanted to be taken advantage of. I always felt that he enjoyed the pleasure of giving, but not of hearing someone say, "I want."

A few days before he died, he told me that he was going to have a diamond "TLC" chain made for me. I replied that he should not waste his money because I'd never had my plain one off and wouldn't take it off for a more expensive one. He commented, "Come on, Mrs. Cocke, let me have a really nice one made for you." To this I replied, "This one is really nice, and I want no other." He had called me at 3:00 a.m. to come out because he was lonely.

Katey in her wedding dress—*From the author's collection.*

10.   Many Reflections

$\mathcal{M}$y association with Elvis where he first mentioned Dee, his father's second wife, was during his first hospitalization. I want to say here that I feel what she has said and written since he went away is how she would have liked for things to be. I can honestly say that I neither buy nor go out of my way to read what she has to say because, from what people who have read it tell me, none of it jives with what he told me. As far as her boys were concerned, Elvis always called them "his father's ex-wife's children." I saw Ricky only a couple of times, and another son I never saw at all. David was around more than the others; he made the trip to Las Vegas with us. I liked him, and Elvis said he was a "pretty good boy, but that he had a temper."

Dee said in one of her statements that they lived at Graceland for a year, but that she wanted her own home. Elvis said to me, "There was no way I was going to let any woman live in my mother's house."

Lisa was quite another story. One night she came upstairs into her room where I was reading. She sat down and wanted to talk. During the conversation she asked two questions: One, was that the only pair of shoes I had, and two, how old was I? I told her I had more shoes, but that I particularly liked these. Then I asked her why she was interested in them. She replied, "Well, those are the only ones you ever wear." The next night, I wore another pair to prove to her that I had more shoes. Elvis got quite a kick out of this. The funniest thing was where my age was concerned. I told her

I was forty-nine, and she said, "Well, I thought that was about how old you were." Then she wanted to know if everyone had as much gray hair as I had when they got to be forty-nine. I told her that some people had gray hair and some didn't. She then wanted to know if her daddy would have gray hair when he got to be as old as I was. I told Lisa that I really doubted that her daddy would ever have gray hair, to which she said, "Well, when I get to be as old as you are, I'm going to dye mine." Her daddy really got a charge out of that, but then he became concerned that she might offend me. I told him that if she did, she and I would talk it out. She really is a sweet little girl and we got along well. She was spoiled by her daddy, but she also was well behaved. In fact, Elvis frequently bragged on Priscilla for how well behaved Lisa was.

The night the *Lisa Marie* was due in town, Elvis asked me if I would be off the following day and I told him no. He said that all of the gang was anxious to see and go up in the plane, but if I had to work the following day he would postpone the trip. I told him I would be off the day after, so he just said okay. That night we had our usual visit, and he went in to dress to go out. He was going out almost nightly to play racquet ball and to a movie. As he left, he came back by my room to say goodnight and tell me he'd see me in the morning before I left for work. The next morning I was having a cup of coffee in my room as I got ready for work when he came in really laughing. I asked what was up, and he said that when they had left the house the night before, everyone thought they were going to the airport; when they passed the cutoff to the airport, the howls went up to see the plane, but he told them no — with no reason given. He asked again if I would be off the next day, and I told him yes and he said okay.

That night when I got to the house, we had our usual visit over the coffee pot. I ordered his breakfast and after he ate, we sat there for another hour or so and talked. He asked me if I was ready to "go up," I said sure, so he went in to get dressed. I went downstairs ahead of him. When I went into the kitchen where all the gang was sitting around drinking coffee, they noticed me with my jacket on and said, "Yipee, we're gonna fly tonight." And did we fly. We had a great time. The plane was filled to capacity. Those there included Vernon, Sandy Miller, Dr. Nick and Edna, Dawn (the girl Elvis dated a few times), plus all of the guys. Linda was in Los Angeles so she missed the maiden voyage. Can you believe that Elvis waited until I could more conveniently go before he took everyone up? That was just one of the many ways he showed his thoughtfulness. Another was the way he never left the house at night without coming by my room just before he left to say goodnight.

Two nights after our whiz-bang trip to Fort Worth, Las Vegas, and Palm Springs, Elvis came into Lisa's room. Linda was there perched up on the corner of Lisa's bed, and I was on the day bed, my favorite place to sit. Elvis sat down in his chair, looked at me very seriously, and said, "Mrs. Cocke, I know how you feel

139

about me and how you feel about my doing things for you, but I don't want you to say one word, understand?" I answered, "Okay," believing he was about to tell me that he didn't need me to come out anymore. Imagine my surprise when he handed me a generous check, plus another check for Katey. The tears flowed that night!

Just a few days before Elvis went away, he called me at 3:00 a.m. one morning to ask me to come out. Usually before he left town on a tour he would call to say goodbye, and frequently he would ask if I could come out before he left. This time I asked him if anything was wrong because usually when he called it was in the late afternoon and he would say, "Would you give me the pleasure of your company for awhile?"

He said there was nothing wrong, that he was lonely and his eyes were hurting. Despite the early hour of the morning, I got up and drove to Graceland as I had always done in the past. When I arrived, he was sitting up in his bed and looking forlorn. He hugged me and said my being there made him feel better. I sat with him until after 6:00 a.m. when he said he felt he could go to sleep, so I left and went back home. The last thing he said to me as I walked out the door was, "The gates of Graceland and the door to this house will always be open to you."

11. Medications

$\mathcal{E}$ lvis was on a number of medications. I do not remember the exact medication that he received, but he was getting medication for hypertension, his colon problem, and (as well as I remember) a medication to keep his heart rate down to normal. All of these medications were what a doctor would give to any patient who had the same health problems Elvis had.

When he was first admitted to the hospital under my care, he was having discomfort and did receive a narcotic — by injection — for this pain. He was monitored, as are all patients receiving this medication, and his was ordered "every four hours PRN." PRN means "when necessary." Thus it is very important that "PRN" be inscribed after the "four hours"; otherwise it means that a patient is to receive the medication every four hours, not just when necessary. His definitely was PRN.

There were several times when he would have the medication every four hours, as the doctor's order was written, but there were just as many times when he would not have the injection for a long period of time because he was not feeling enough pain to take it. Even before he left the hospital, this narcotic was pretty much a thing of the past, and he was receiving only the standard medications ordered for his colon problem, not any narcotic.

Shortly after I began going to Graceland, there was a flare-up of his colon problem and his cramping pain returned. Dr. Nick brought us some codeine tablets which Kathy and I carefully monitored, keeping a list of when we gave them and counting them twice daily. We never came up short in our count. The codeine did not agree with Elvis, and we had to ask Dr. Nick for another type of medication. This also was charted and accounted for daily by us, and it was necessary to administer it only for two or three days.

Elvis required medication in order to get to sleep more than for anything else. Remember that he was a big man, and often we gave him two sleeping capsules where an average (smaller) man might have required only one. There were times when he would come in several hours later, wide awake, and ask for another sleeping pill. This kind of thing can happen anytime, anyplace, with any patient. When he would be out all night playing racquet ball and going to a movie and was not home before I left to go to the hospital, I would put out a "doggie bag" for him. This bag held the medication for his blood pressure and his colon problem, which he was to take that morning, as well as sleeping medication he could take if he needed it. Usually he did take it, but sometimes it would still be on his bedside table when I got there in the evening.

Elvis ate a lot of salt on his food. Salt causes the retention of fluids in the body, and the amount he ate contributed greatly to making him puffy. We had a medication to make him eliminate some of this fluid — the same medication that thousands of people take every day — but it made him feel weak. One day when we were talking about his puffiness, he told me that the medication sapped his strength so much that he felt bad after taking it. He found the puffiness easier to tolerate than the weakness. We got a salt substitute for him, and he used it a lot. Often, however, he would still use the regular salt because he said it tasted better.

At no time during the months I spent at Graceland did I ever see any type of narcotic or barbiturate that was not prescribed by Dr. Nick for some specific problem, and these Dr. Nick gave strict orders about administering. However, if there were other medication ordered by another physician we were not aware of them, and such a thing happening would be very difficult for me to believe as there was never a time I saw Elvis when he appeared to be under the influence of drugs. Dr. Nick was very devoted to Elvis and extremely concerned about his welfare. He was very protective of him and cared for him as he would a younger brother. We followed Dr. Nick's specific instructions, and there was never a time that I noted any sort of medication abuse or misuse. As I previously stated, Kathy Seamon and I carefully monitored all his medications, regardless of what they were. There were no needle marks on his body other than the few we put there, and the skin on his arms and legs was unbroken.

Let me tell another thing about Elvis. He was difficult to stick for any type of lab work, as he was very muscular and his veins were deeply embedded and small. I learned this when he was first admitted to my care in January of 1975. He had been in the hospital before I met him, and he knew Estelle Claiborne, who was in charge of the lab pick-up team. When a blood sample was needed, we called her. Elvis said that she was the only person who had ever been able to stick him, and he was right. She was certainly the expert and was able to obtain blood samples when no one else could.

I saw this demonstrated on one occasion. One day one of the residents told Elvis that he could stick him, and he had brought the necessary items. I stood watching. The resident probed and Elvis never batted an eye, but I squirmed and gripped my hands behind my back until I couldn't stand to watch any more. Finally I walked out, called Estelle, and she came immediately and drew the necessary blood on the first try. Elvis said later, "If you have to have any more lab work, you be sure you get Mrs. Claiborne, because nobody else is going to stick me!"

Another thing I have often heard concerning his health is that he ate nothing but junk food. This was not true. When he was in the hospital, Carol Kidney, the dietician, came to visit Elvis daily. She would come up every morning, talk to him about his meals, and get his requests for the day. She made various suggestions about some of his requests, and he was very cooperative in every way. He usually ate pretty much the same thing and didn't want a lot of variety, but nevertheless, he ate well. He would usually have strawberries, bacon, eggs, toast (which he ate sparingly), and coffee for breakfast. Lunch and dinner were about the same usually; he wanted hamburger steaks, creamed potatoes, string beans or spinach, and a salad. Sometimes he asked for a bacon burger and hash browns at night, but that certainly was not "junk food."

Carol always tried to vary his tray, when possible, and she spent a lot of time seeing that he got not only what he liked, but also what he needed. We have a great dietary department, and they certainly went all out for Elvis as they do for all patients.

At Graceland I never noticed him eating junk food. He was careful about his diet and usually ate balanced meals.

The coroner's report stated that Elvis died of a heart attack and that he had an enlarged heart. This was no surprise to me. Elvis had the biggest heart of anyone I've ever known. He was both generous and compassionate, and his love for people was tremendous. Thus this seems the appropriate way for him to have gone. In my opinion, he had one other fatal illness — loneliness.

12.   Elvis Goes Away

The morning of August 16, 1977, the phone rang in my office around 8 a.m. It was Delta saying Elvis wanted me to drop by before he left. We talked for a couple of minutes, and I hung up. About twenty minutes later the phone rang again. It was Elvis, and he wanted to know if Aunt Delta had called me. I said yes, and he asked if I could come out before he left. I said I'd be off at 3:00 p.m. and would come out then. He told me he had four tickets for me to the concert to be held the night he got back to town, and he said he was going to read awhile and get some sleep.

Around 3:00 p.m. I was once again in my office when I heard the "Harvey Team" being paged for the E. R. The HT is what is always called for a person who has had a cardiac arrest, and the operator paged many times. I thought, "Gee, I hope they make it in time." I went to the nursing office where I found I was being paged "stat." I answered and found it was 5118, which I knew to be Maurice Elliott's office. I called, and Carolyn Pulliam told me that the "HT" was for Elvis. I hung up and immediately left for the Emergency Room.

When I walked—no ran—into the E.R., I saw Charlie Hodge and Joe Esposito. Charlie hugged me and said it looked bad, and I went to pieces. He and Joe, along with the ER supervisor, Annett Bingham, got me into an empty room for a few minutes. She said I should go in her office, so they took me there. When I was able to compose myself, I said I was going to where Elvis was.

When I got in the room, John Quartermous was doing cardio-pulmonary resuscitation. The room was full, and Dr. Nick was there. He just looked at me, as did John. I read what was in their faces because I couldn't really see Elvis. Owen Taylor, one of the residents, knew that I always took care of Elvis, so he came around the room, stood beside me, and put his arm around me. He asked if I was sure I wanted to stay in there. I said yes, so he just held on tighter and held me up. I reached out and touched one of the interns on the arm and moved him aside so I could see Elvis. When I did, my knees got weak, and Owen held on tighter. I said, "Please stop." It was evident that the soul of this boy had long since left his body, and I could not bear to see them continue. John looked over at Dr. Nick. He told him to hold up on the CPR, and when he saw that there was absolutely no complex on the EKG he agreed that they would stop. He came over and hugged me and we both went out.

My boy was gone . . . .

I went in where the boys were, Joe, Al, Billy and Charlie, and Maurice Elliott. Mr. Elliott asked me if I was okay and I said yes. I stayed with the boys a minute, then went back in the room to get Elvis' pajamas and the chain from around his neck. All of the Harvey Team members had left, and there were two nurses and an attendant preparing his body for transfer to the morgue. His chain and pajamas were gone; they had been secured at the nurses' station. I looked at his precious face. The shock of black hair was over his left eye, and I kissed him on the cheek and left. I stopped at the nurse's station and collected his valuables to take them to Graceland.

Meanwhile, Miss Farnell had arrived in the ER. She took me up to her office and got me a coke. I called the Helen of Memphis Shop where Katey worked and asked to speak to her boss. I asked her to take Katey someplace private and tell her about Elvis; then I called Bob. I got home late. Mrs. Jimmie Wright, one of the assistant directors in nursing service, took me. I couldn't even think about going to Graceland, and I had not wanted to see anyone at the hospital. Mr. Elliott had already received a call to ask if "Elvis' Favorite Nurse" had been in the ER. He gave out no information.

My phone rang at home all night with calls both local and long distance. People came in and out, and I felt as though the rug had been jerked out from under my feet. Katey and Rod, her husband, came over, as did Florine Cocke, my sister-in-law from Clarksdale, Mississippi, on Bob's side of the family, and her daughter, Becky Kelly, who was on her way to Guam to join her husband, Colonel James Kelly, a pilot with SAC. I spent a sleepless night, got up early, and went to work. A short while after I got there, Maurice Elliott called me in my office to see how I was. He told me that I was to feel free to come and go as I chose the rest of the week. I told him I had come early that day as I wanted to leave by noon to go on out to Graceland and that I would be back on Friday. He again told me take as much time as I needed.

I stayed busy all morning, and about 12:00 noon I received a call from Carolyn Pulliam, Mr. Elliott's secretary. She asked if I would mind being interviewed by CBS. I told her I wanted to leave as soon as possible, but if we could do it quickly I would agree. I went down to the administrative offices and was taken to the conference room where I met the cameraman and the lady who was to do the interview. Hospital security was there and stood outside the door as the interview was held. This lasted about twenty minutes, after which I left for Graceland.

What a mob! When I got off the expressway and approached Brooks Road intersection, it was bumper to bumper. I found that if I pulled into the lane for left turn only, I could make excellent time. As I approached the area where I would be turning to go into the back entrance, a policeman on a motorcycle stopped me and told me to get in the regular lane of traffic. I said, "I'm Mrs. Cocke." Before I could explain who I was, he said, "Yes Ma'am, you're expected," so I was ushered in. I drove up to the back of the house, and one of the policemen parked my car.

I went in the back door. Al Strada, Dick Grob, and Billy Smith were in the den. I went on up the steps into the kitchen and met Delta. We hugged each other, and she said, "They have just brought Elvis home. Come on in and see him." The living room had been stripped of all furniture, and folding chairs lined the area. The room was filled with flowers, and at the end of the living room and in the double archway that leads into the music room was the copper casket that held the remains of the boy who had walked into my heart two and one-half years earlier.

I said, "Hi ya, Babe," which was the way I had always greeted him. He was dressed in a white suit, a light blue shirt, and a white silk tie. On his ring finger was his TCB ring with the eleven-carat diamond. The way his hand lay by his side, the ring was barely visible; unless one stood there for a minute or two, it could not be seen. The black hair was combed, and the shock of hair that always fell over the left eye was combed back. I took my fingers and flipped it in place. Then he looked like the boy I had grown to love as I would my own. Delta left me alone with him for a few minutes; then Charlie came in. We talked for a few minutes, and I excused myself.

I went to Grandma's room where Vernon, Nash, Grandma, and Delta were. Dr. Nick was there also, as was Elias Ganno from Vegas. I stayed in there for about thirty minutes, then went out for a cup of coffee. I went in through the dining room with my cup and put it on the table so I could go sign the register. There was a slight girl with long, light brown hair at the book, writing her name, and as she turned I saw it was Priscilla. She immediately put her arms around me and said, "Oh, Mrs. Cocke, thank you so very much. Elvis loved you, and you were so good to him." We both cried, and I said, "Thank you for that. He loved you too."

Most of the rest of that day was pretty hectic. The doors were opened at 3:00 p.m., and the public was invited to view the body. I was kept busy outside with fainting and screaming women, as were many other people. I stayed in this capacity for over two hours, then went back in the house and sat with Priscilla at the dining room table.

Around 5:00 p.m. I went back to Grandma's room and told Delta that I felt I needed to leave so they could have some privacy. She asked me not to, so I stayed in with them for another hour or so. As dark began to fall, she then said to go so I would get home before complete dark set in, but please to come back in the morning. The funeral was for 2:00 p.m. I went out the back gate as I had come in, stopping to tell the policeman on duty to go to the house and eat. As I drove down the back road heading into the highway, I was faced with a mob that wouldn't break a place in line to let me through. I had to back up the road and ask one of the motorcycle police men to get me out, which he did.

The next morning I showered and dressed, went by the beauty shop, and headed back to Graceland, arriving around 9:00 a.m. I had worn a white dress because Elvis did not like black. He preferred white, and I would not go to his funeral in black.

I again drove in the left turn only lane, but was known by then and didn't have to give my name. The policeman had to clear the way for me to get to the back road, but there were no problems otherwise. When I got in the back gate and drove to the house, I once again parked in the back and left my keys in the car in case it was necessary to move it. I went into the kitchen, nodded to Vernon, and went into the dining room where I sat down to drink a cup of coffee. Sandy came into the dining room and asked me to come sit with Vernon for a few minutes which I did, as he wanted to talk to me. Sandy Miller is a nurse who takes care of Vernon. She is truly a fine person and has been so good for him. Elvis was very fond of her and always appreciated her devotion to his father.

I went into the kitchen, sat with Vernon for a short while, then got another cup of coffee and went on to Grandma's room. I stayed with her until a couple of her grandchildren came in. Then I went to say my final and private goodbye to Elvis. I knew this would be my last time to be alone with him. Sandy Miller was by the bier when I went in and we spoke briefly, after which she left. For the last time I said, "Hi ya, Babe." I talked to him for a few minutes, told him how much he meant to me, stroked his cheek, kissed him on the forehead, and walked away. He was my kid, my friend, my confidant. We had laughed together and cried together many times. I could shed no more tears because I knew that he was safe now. No one or nothing else could ever hurt him again — and he had been hurt many times in the past. He had been betrayed by people he called friend, he had been slandered by those who envied him, and he had been taken advantage of because of his generous nature. Nothing else could touch him now.

The funeral services were in good taste, the music beautiful, and the eulogies what he deserved. I rode to the cemetery in the white Cadillac which preceded the hearse. The director and I had spent quite awhile talking that morning. He knew of my close friendship, so he told me to ride with him, which I did. Never have I seen such a tribute to a man. The whole world knows of this, so there is no need to put it down on paper. After the services ended at the mausoleum, we returned to Graceland with a police escort.

As I went into the house, Vernon preceded me into the dining room. He called to me, and I went in to sit with him for a few minutes. I thanked him for allowing me to be a part of the last two days, and in a voice that sounded just like Elvis he said, "You're very welcome, Mrs. Cocke."

I got a cup of coffee and went into the den. A woman sat down next to me and said, "I surely would like to ask for his autograph." I asked, "Whose?" She said, "George Hamilton." When I admitted that I didn't know who George Hamilton was, she replied, "The movie star," and pointed him out to me. I had seen him when I first had walked in, but did not know who he was. When I had first seen him, I thought, "Who in the heck is that turkey that doesn't have any better sense than to go around with his shirt unbuttoned, showing his chest, and his sleeves rolled up." Needless to say, he didn't impress me in the least.

I had noticed a red-haired lady at the funeral with a tall, nice-looking man, but I didn't know until I saw their picture in the paper the following day that it was Ann-Margret and Roger Smith. There were reports that John Wayne, Sammy Davis, Jr., and other stars would be there, but they were not.

It was a pity that Caroline Kennedy came — not to offer her condolences, but to gape and sell a story. She spent only about ten minutes in the house, and when she did write her story the details she gave were not accurate. She should have saved herself a trip and stayed home.

There were many people about, going into the kitchen for food and just standing around talking in general. I was sickened by this, for I felt that the family needed less confusion. Therefore I went to Grandma's room and told her goodbye. She asked if I had to leave, and I told her yes — and that, hopefully, when I did about two hundred others would follow me and the family could get some rest.

I said my goodbyes to the rest of the family and left. As I approached each cluster of uniformed policemen, national guardsmen, sheriff's deputies, etc., I stopped and thanked them for their kindness. A policeman, Lieutenant Holmes, came up and said, "Elvis loved you, Mrs. Cocke." He said he had seen me on television the night before and knew that I loved Elvis too.

I still go to Graceland, visit Grandma and Delta, and have lunch with them. Occasionally, and always after the fans leave, I go to the gravesite and spend a few quiet moments alone. The area is beautiful and was one of his favorite places. I know that only the shell of the man rests under that impressive and beautifully sculptured marble slab. The soul has long since left that shell.

In time to come, as you read this, I hope I have conveyed to you the Elvis I knew. He was a good man, a kind man, a generous man, and a loving man. He never forgot his upbringing. Many times he spoke of those "lean years." The greatest pleasure he got out of life was in doing for other people, and I truly doubt that anyone, anywhere, could ever match him in generosity and kindness. Oh, I don't mean in what he gave his friends — the material things — I mean in what he gave the world: the benefits he did, the people he helped in hospitals, the bills he paid for people he didn't even know, the man who told me one night, "Sometimes I think the one thing that would please me the most would be to give all of this away and walk through that gate with my daddy, in overalls and barefooted, but free."

Babe, to live in the hearts of those you love and leave behind is not to die.

Epilog

Memories of a Legend

My friend, Ryan Tracy, a Memphian now, but formerly from Shelbyville, Kentucky was at my house for dinner one Sunday night, and when I told him that my book had gone into reprint-he said "That's great – did you write a final chapter?" to which I said, "No.", so he told me that I should have, so here 'tis.

AND THE YEARS HAVE GONE BY BUT THE MEMORY AND LEGEND OF ELVIS PRESLEY GOES ON

It has been almost 32 years since Elvis Presley moved from his home in Memphis to God's House - - my how the years have flown by. I remember when he died, some goofy guy made the remark that in a year they won't remember his name. I don't know where the goofy guy is, but I can tell you this; ELVIS PRESLEY IS ALIVE AND WELL IN THE HEARTS OF THOSE HE LEFT BEHIND!!-

Much has been done to keep the memory of this special young man alive, and I am sure that I will not get a lot of things in this little "follow up", because when I became thirty-nine, forty-four years ago, for some reason or other, my memory has not been the very best, but I'm going to try.

Fan clubs have worked very hard throughout the years, and they choose charities to support just as Elvis did. To name a few of these that I personally can remember, True Fans for Elvis in Maine, the EP Continentals in Orlando - (the only club name by Elvis), the Rock-A-Hula fan club in California, the Jail House Rockers in California, the Elvis Happy Fan Club in New Jersey, the Elvis Fan-tesy Fest in Portage, Indiana, and We Remember Elvis from Pittsburgh. Darwin Lamm publishes the EIF magazine, which is world-wide, and he puts on great shows as tributes to Elvis, and thru these, he does his part in charity support. Graceland, well, they are unbelievable with all that they do to continue to come up with all that they plan and do for the fans to show their appreciation. Yes, my friends, Elvis is Alive and Well, and thru you, and our children to come, this wonderful man will remain in our history books, as well as in our hearts, for many decades to come

I miss Elvis. There isn't a day that goes by that I don't think of him. I play his music in my car, and I go to sleep with his gospels, but I miss our nightly chats. I miss the days he would call and say, "Can you come after work and have a cup of coffee and give me a back rub?", "Can you come out for a visit?", etc., but most of all, I think that I remember our last few moments together. Elvis called me at 2AM to see if I would come out and sit with him, he was tired, he couldn't sleep and he needed me to come though Ginger was there.

I went. I sat on the side of the bed till around 6:30; sat quietly with my hand on his and finally he said "You can go home now Ms Cocke, I can go to sleep now." and as I walked to the door he said, "Ms Cocke?" I turned to him and said, "What honey?" and he said, "The doors of this house will always be open to you." I had no idea that this would be the last time I was to see him face to face. Had I realized that in the next few days he would be gone, I would never have left. Now when I watch one of his movies, listen to a CD, or play a DVD and see him in his magnificence, I feel something that is indescribable. I wish that I could describe it. Perhaps it is as though I am covered with a soft warm blanket for comfort. I don't know, but for this gentle spirit who entered my life and taught me much about the joy of living and of giving, I look with awe, respect and admiration. Was Elvis different from other guys I've known? Elvis was different from anyone I've ever known, and I can tell you this; once this young man touched your life as he touched mine, you are never the same again. You will not forget him. You will ever carry him in your heart, but remember this too, and he would tell you this, there is only one king, and that is Jesus Christ. He did not want nor expect anyone to worship or idolize him. He just wanted to be loved and respected for himself.

Let's talk about other folks too, and bring you up to date on some of them. George Klein is one who has done so much to keep the memory and the legend of this young man alive. He is tireless in his dedication and his devotion. George is a gentle, lovable puppy to me, and I love and respect this young man for himself and for the way that he continues to TCB. Jerry Schilling , my pick of the litter, has also been a part of keeping the legend alive, and he too, like George, continues to be a busy man. Dick Grob, Sam Thompson, and Joe Esposita all live in Vegas, yet all come to Memphis from time to time, and they too, keep on TCB'n. DJ Fontana is such a sweetheart and though his health hasn't been the greatest in the world, is out there at every opportunity to talk about Elvis and to "beat those sticks"!! Scotty Moore has pretty much retired. I think that old arthritis got into hands and made it hard to play that guitar. Gordon Stoker and Ray Walker are two of the greatest men I know, and I have known them for many years. Luis Nunley and Curtis Young came later, but they are good men and donate their time, their talent, and their love and energy into the Elvis Presley Memorial Dinner each year to make it the success that it has been. JD Summer and the Stamps have sung for this event, too. And goodness, how we miss JD who won the hearts of millions.

Thru the years, Sam Phillips, JD, Richard Davis, Charlie Hodge, Alan Fortas, Boots Randolph and others have gone to the other side. Al Davorin, Mister, "ELVIS HAS LEFT THE BUILDING" man, Otis Blackwell who wrote Don't Be Cruel and others, James Blackwood and Cecil Blackwood, who were in the original Blackwood Brothers Quartet, and all of the ladies who worked for Elvis, Pauline Nicholson, Lottie and Mary Jenkins , all great ladies, all great cooks, all loved "Mr P". Stan Kessler from the old days is still around and lives in Memphis, though he is in poor health. He wrote, Baby Lets Play House, I'm Right and Your Left, She Gone, and other songs for Elvis. Larry Geller and his wife Shira continue to live in LA, and Mark and Karen James are well and continue to live between Nashville and LA. Bill Morris and his wife Ann live in Memphis.

Of Elvis family, his dad Vernon, his uncle Vester, and his aunts Delta, Gladys, and Nash have all gone to the other side, as has Patsey's husband Clifton, and uncle Earl.

Priscilla and Lisa Marie continue with the legacy and legend of Elvis. Priscilla devotes a great bit of her time to charitable works, as does Lisa Marie. Just look at the Presley Place and go on from there! Both of these ladies have always been very dear to me, after all, Lisa and I were once "roommates" during my stint at Graceland and I hold them very close to my heart.

165

In my own family, since all of these friends moved on, my family have followed; mother left just before Elvis left, my youngest sister, Patty, my dad, Howard Justice, my oldest brother, Dick, and my youngest brother Joe. When we were coming home from Virginia after Joe died, my daughter, Katey, said, "Mother I wonder who will be next?" She was. Katey made her step into the other side a year later on July 5, 2001, and on May 22, 2006, Bob followed. From my immediate family, only my sister, Catherine remains, and she lives in Dallas with her daughter, Sally, while I continue to reside in Memphis with Katey's puppy, Buttons, who will be 15 on Kateys 56th birthday this year. Buttons is a great and loving companion but she doesn't talk much!

I retired from nursing the second time in 2004 after another 16 years at Baptist Memorial Hospital. I teach a Stephen Ministry Class at my church two nights a month, along with three other leaders. I work a half a day a week at church as a volunteer and attend a weekly bible study on Wednesday nights. When I'm not doing these things, I just try to stay out of trouble, which at my age is not easy! I attend church on Sunday and am a life elder. I do very little outside work because of health limitations, but Nancy and her crew from church, along with my friends, Priscilla, Barbara, and Onie, who help out when they are in town, keep my back garden looking beautiful.

I have been blessed with good friends. My Elvis friends are among my closest and dearest, and I treasure these friendships. During the long illness of both Katey and Bob, it was my Elvis friends who came and were there for me; my friends from Graceland, my friends from Orlando, Prisicilla, Barbara, Sue, Vince, Onie, Paul, Tony and Chris, Donna and Karen and Bill, along with other parts of the country. My Elvis friends are my family - all of you. I can only ask one last thing of each of you. Through your love and support of Elvis, KEEP HIM ALIVE for generations to come. He and his music will remain in your hearts. He knew his ability came from God, and that you were his loving fans who made him known throughout the world.

Elvis asked me one night, "Ms Cocke, do you think the fans will remember me when I'm gone?" I told him, "Yes", and you have once again, proven me right.

TLC
Marian

To Order: - Contact - Marian Cocke
784 Pecan Gardens CL East
Memphis, TN 38122
Ph - 901-324-9612
email - epnurse@bellsouth.net

All books personally autographed